POACHERS, LIES AND ALIBIS

POACHERS, LIES AND ALIBIS

By

William Wasserman

Copyright © June 2019 by Penn's Woods Publications

A Penn's Woods Book

All rights reserved. This book or parts thereof must not be reproduced in any form without permission in writing from the publisher. For information, address Penn's Woods Publications, 38 Ganibrille Ct., Simpsonville, SC 29681

ISBN: 978-0-578-52049-0

Cover by John Wasserman

A special thank you to Bob Fala, Mike Schmit and Tim Grenoble for helping to provide the photographs in this book.

ALSO BY WILLIAM WASSERMAN

Poacher Hunter

It's a Wild Life

Track of the Poacher

Wildlife Guardian

Game Warden

Poacher Wars

Trapping Secrets

Pennsylvania Wildlife Tails

For Jeff Pierce, deputy extraordinaire!
You were always there for me.

Introduction

For more than thirty years, I tracked down outlaw hunters and brought them to justice. From the big city streets of Philadelphia to the rugged mountains of northern Pennsylvania, I pursued them on foot and by vehicle and by boat. Along the way, I investigated thousands of game law violations and arrested many career poachers.

My patrol districts comprised roughly four hundred square miles where I encountered some of the most unpredictable characters under the sun. Some were likable, others were despicable, but they all had one thing in common: a blatant disregard for our natural resource laws and a sense of fair play.

This book centers on my early years as a state game warden where I talk about my training at the Ross Leffler School of Conservation and my first assigned district working as an urban game warden for thirteen years. The incidents recounted in this book are real; however, the stories are based on my memories over a period of years and may differ from the memories of others. I admit to taking some creative liberties with events and to re-creating some of the dialog. I have also given the poachers and their associates fictitious names and have altered their physical descriptions. Any resemblance to actual persons, living or dead, is entirely coincidental.

Choose a job you love, and you will never have to work a day in your life.
　　— Confucius

Make the boy interested in natural history if you can; it is better than games; they encourage it in some schools.
~Robert Falcon Scott

In the Beginning

So, HOW DID IT ALL BEGIN? Perhaps many of you have wondered, after reading my stories over the years, what made me decide to become a state game warden. I guess you could say it all started with my love of the outdoors, which began as soon as I was old enough to leave the confines of my suburban back yard and start exploring the natural world around me. I was nine years old at the time, living in Delaware County, Pennsylvania with my mother, father, twin brother and sister.

It was back in 1957, and I loved to roam the fields and streams around my home, hunting for frogs, snakes and turtles. The frogs I caught were promptly released, for I knew they had to stay moist to survive. Besides, I had no place to keep them back at home. Same for the snakes. Mom wouldn't let me in the house if I brought a snake home, which I often did. "Look, Mom!" I'd say proudly as I stood at the front door with the steely-eyed serpent slithering from hand to hand. "Isn't it beautiful!"

Mom would step back from the front door and force a tense smile. "Yes, Billy," she'd say. "It's beautiful. Now, why don't you take it back in the woods and let it go." Of course, I knew that was coming, and I would promptly do an about-face and carry the snake back to where I found it.

I had pretty good success with box turtles as pets because I could keep them outside in my back yard. After building a corral of rocks, I'd place the turtle in the enclosure along with a small bowl of water to drink. Then I'd run off and dig up some worms for its supper. I'd hold them in in front of its impassive face, one by one, until the turtle would stretch its leathery neck toward the dangling worm, slowly rotate its head for a sideward bite, and snatch it in prehistoric jaws. When I couldn't find enough worms, I'd take some raw hamburger from the fridge and an occasional piece of celery or lettuce for it to eat. Eventually, the turtle would simply climb over my shallow rock wall and escape. Probably all for the best, as it needed to be free, like all wild creatures.

When I was twelve, we moved to a rural area in Bucks County where I became interested in hunting and trapping, with muskrats taking precedence over squirrels and pheasants.

Bill with a morning's catch of muskrats in 1961.

By the time I grew into my mid-teens, I found myself spending all of my free time setting traps for muskrats, raccoons and foxes while dreaming of becoming a professional trapper in the wilds of Alaska.

That all changed when I met my wife, Maryann, back in 1966. We were married a few years later, and I knew a life in the wilderness wouldn't have suited her. She loved her friends and family and wanted to stay close to them, so I began looking for work in Bucks County where we both grew up.

For the next five years, I drifted from job to job, working mostly in construction while running an early morning trapline during the fall and winter months with my brother, John. We both dreamed of finding jobs working with wildlife, but they were hard to come by, and what few were available required a college degree, which neither of us had.

In 1974, my brother and I applied for positions as deputies with Bill Lockett, the state game warden assigned to Bucks County. He appointed both of us. As such, we had the same powers of arrest and enforcement as full-time officers while serving as non-salaried volunteers. We were provided uniforms and Game Law books, but had to purchase our own firearms, emergency radio equipment and other essential gear, as well as use our personal vehicles for patrol.

I had a 1953 Willys jeep, which enabled me to go just about anywhere off-road. The steepest mountain grades were no challenge for the little four-runner, and it could crawl over dry creek beds littered with boulder-sized rocks as if it were walking on legs. Because it was unmarked, like the official state vehicles used by salaried officers, I was able to get up close and personal with more than a few outlaw hunters.

From September through January, my brother, John and I spent every weekend patrolling the rolling countryside of upper Bucks County. We worked primarily with other deputies, which is how we received most of our early training. Night patrol was a regular part of our vigil, and we spent many cold nights nestled into some obscure overlook, observing the valleys below for poaching activity.

We soon discovered that hunting poachers was an exciting and rewarding avocation, so when the Pennsylvania State Civil Service Commission announced a test for full-time employment as a state game warden the following year, John and I immediately applied for positions. But when we learned that there were over two thousand additional applicants and only thirty openings, our hearts sank. The odds of making it into the Training School seemed dismal at best. Having no military experience meant we did not qualify for veterans' preference, which added ten additional points to their examination score. Additionally, military veterans who were among the top candidates were given mandatory preference in hiring over non-veterans, but they could also be appointed over non-veterans regardless of their rank on the list. John and I also had no college degrees to boost our odds of getting in, and we knew many applicants would be college graduates with degrees in wildlife management, forestry and biology.

Although both of us had attended college a few years back, we dropped out after the first year. Neither of us liked being cooped up in a school all day. Our high school days had seemed like an eternity until we finally graduated twelfth grade. But we decided to give college a try, thinking our attitudes toward school life might change. It did not, and although it was during the height of the Vietnam War, when body counts of our soldiers and marines were announced on the radio every day, we both quit college knowing we'd be drafted into the military. What we didn't know was how fast that would happen, for within two short weeks we got our draft notices and reported to a Military Processing Station in

Philadelphia to be examined by a doctor for physical qualifications prior to induction into the Armed Forces.

As it turned out, John had a medical condition he was unaware of, which kept him out of the Armed Forces, and I was being treated by a doctor for internal injuries sustained in a car crash two months earlier. It happened when John and I were on our way to college and were involved in a head-on collision with an International Harvester Scout. It was the first snow of the year, and the three-thousand-pound Scout rounded a bend too fast, lost control, and slid directly into my brother's 1962 Ford Galaxy. Both cars were totally destroyed. After obtaining my physical records from the doctor who was treating me, the military excused me from the draft.

It had been eight years since I graduated high school, and now, with no Veteran's preference or college degree to help me, I was looking at a four-hour written Civil Service test for the game warden position with a mandatory passing grade of eighty percent or above. And that would be just the beginning. If I managed to get a passing grade, there would be oral interviews and physical exams to hurdle. As a lifelong outdoorsman, I wasn't worried about questions regarding wildlife or natural resources, and as a deputy game warden, I had studied our state game laws and was certain I could answer questions regarding hunting and trapping regulations. But I wasn't confident about questions on math, English and history, as my grades in high school weren't so hot, especially in math, and I'd been out of school too long to remember much about it. So to better prepare, I went to a bookstore and purchased a pile of manuals to help me freshen my memory on the subjects I'd studied in school, and spent the next six months studying for the test.

Written examinations were scheduled at various locations throughout the state to accommodate the two-thousand-and-some-odd applicants, and when Examination Day finally came, I found myself walking into a spacious high school auditorium in lower Bucks County. There were about fifty men standing around inside, waiting to be assigned to a room for the test. They split us into two groups, each with a separate room. Once inside, we were fingerprinted by a local police officer. Those who were eventually selected for the Game Commission Training School would be fingerprinted again to be certain no one had someone else take the test for them, as well as for criminal background checks. Exam questions ranged from general math, spelling and vocabulary to natural history and Pennsylvania game laws. I spent the entire four hours of allotted time on the test, carefully going over my answers once finished, to make sure I had everything in order. When the final buzzer rang, prompting the few remaining applicants to turn in their papers, I felt confident of a passing grade, but had no idea if I scored high enough to be called for further testing.

I waited six long weeks before a letter with a return address from the Pennsylvania Civil Service Commission arrived in my mailbox. My heart pounded as I stood at the mailbox and tore open the envelope. Miraculously, it seemed, at least to me, I had passed with a high grade, and I breathed a huge sigh of relief knowing I'd made it over the first hurdle. As I read on, I learned that applicants with the top three hundred test scores would be scheduled for oral examinations several months later in Harrisburg. I stuffed the letter into my back pocket and ran into the house to call my brother. John confirmed that he too had passed the written exam and was also scheduled for an oral interview.

It was rather intimidating to walk into a dimly lit conference room with three strangers in the upper echelon of state government staring down at you. Two were in Game Commission uniforms while the third wore the uniform of a Pennsylvania State Trooper. They were seated side-by-side at a long table. A flinty-eyed Game Commission officer with a gray crew cut motioned for me to sit across from them. I tried to look relaxed. Tried to look self-confident. But in reality, I had to struggle to control the jitters I felt welling up inside of me. But it was do-or-die time, so I steeled myself, making sure to look each officer in the eye when they addressed me. They took turns, the questions starting off easy enough: Why do you want to be a game warden? Why do you feel qualified for this position? Have you ever been in trouble with the law? What is your present occupation?—that sort of thing. But after a few minutes things changed and the questions they asked became much more difficult. Some didn't seem to have a suitable answer, while others put you in a hypothetical dilemma—with two choices, each of them bad. But you persevered, did your best, and somehow managed to get through it all.

Then you waited again.

Months passed until you were notified by mail, the letter stating that they had whittled the candidate selection down to a final forty applicants chosen for additional oral tests and a physical examination in Harrisburg. I couldn't help but think the odds were against twin brothers making it into the Training School, and that bothered me a lot. John and I are identical twins with a unique relationship that most siblings can't know. I wanted my brother to be accepted into the school as much as I wanted it for myself, and I know John felt the same way. Our oral interviews were scheduled on the same day. We had a month to prepare, then it was off to southcentral Pennsylvania for a physical exam (easy part) and one more oral interview. The big one. The one that would determine success or failure for both of us.

The interview took place at Game Commission Headquarters in Harrisburg. Once again, I steeled myself for more questions as a uniformed game warden escorted me down a long hallway leading into a small office. Sitting at a desk, was a middle-aged game warden with reddish-brown hair and ice-blue eyes. He stuck out a hand and we shook briefly. He offered me a seat. There was a single chair directly in front of his desk. I sat down, folded my hands, and waited for him to begin. My heart was beating so hard I wondered if he could hear it. There were thirty openings for the position, which meant only ten people in the entire world now separated me from a career with the Pennsylvania Game Commission. I tried not to think about that too much. I tried not to think about that and the miserable fact that I could blow everything in the next few minutes simply by answering one key question the wrong way!

And then it began: What were my feelings on the Commission's pheasant stocking program? Did I think farm-raised birds weakened the wild birds through interbreeding? Knowing I was a trapper from southeastern Pennsylvania, he asked what I thought of the organized fox hunters (called red coats by many, they chased foxes from horseback with trained foxhounds) who were vehemently opposed to fox trapping? How did I feel about the proposal for raccoon hunting season to start two weeks before the trapping season? Did I think it was unfair? Suppose I were to catch a poacher who knew something about my past and threatened to use the information against me...would I let him go or would I arrest him?

On and on he went with his questions. They came off the top of his head; there was no prewritten list. He didn't need one. He was that good. I answered as best I could, constantly fearful that he might rise from his chair at any moment with an immense, toothy grin...

Oh my!

...and say, "DO YOU REALLY EXPECT ME TO HIRE SOMEBODY WITH DOPEY ANSWERS LIKE THAT?"

But he did not. In fact, he was pretty laid-back, albeit pokerfaced, and I really couldn't tell what he was thinking, although by the time the interview was over I had warmed up quite a bit and thought I did well.

Another month passed when I got a phone call from the Commission's Regional Headquarters near Reading, informing me that two Game Commission Officers would be stopping by my house to speak with my wife and me about a career with the agency. After setting up a day and time that was convenient for all, I hung up the phone and breathed a sigh of relief thinking I must have made it into the top thirty candidates for the school.

When the officers showed up at my house the following week, I was told that the Game Commission hadn't narrowed the field down as of yet. I was still in the top forty. Although they had a number of questions for me, I soon realized that the interview was just as much about my wife, Maryann, as it was about me when they told her I could be assigned anywhere in the state and asked how she felt about the possibility of moving from southeastern Pennsylvania, three hundred miles away, to Erie County. And by the way, love your house, looks brand new. How do you feel about moving? In the end, she held up rather well (having managed to put off fainting until after they left) and I was very proud of her.

Finally, after eight exhausting months of tests, interviews and examinations, I received a certified letter from the Pennsylvania Game Commission stating that I had been selected to the Ross Leffler School of Conservation, commonly called the Training School—the only one of its kind in the world at that time. It said I was to contact the Game Commission within three days and advise if I was interested.

Interested...? Excited, elated, euphoric would be more like it. I put the letter on the kitchen counter, picked up the phone with shaking hands and dialed the number at the bottom of the letter, informing the voice on the other end that I'd be there (even if I had to walk the two hundred sixty miles to the school I thought). Next I called my brother, John to see if he got a letter too. Since the first Training School in 1935, brothers had never been accepted to the same class before, let alone twins. So when John told me he was also accepted to the school I was thrilled.

There has always been a lot of competition for jobs in the conservation field. Whether it be forestry, park ranger, conservation agent, game warden, fish warden or what have you, these jobs are scarce and at the same time sought after by many thousands nationwide. In our case, the Pennsylvania Game Commission had slowly whittled the initial two thousand applicants down to thirty men. John and I felt very fortunate.

The Training School was built in 1915 as a hunting lodge for a group of wealthy attorneys. It was purchased by the Game Commission and opened its doors to the first class of game wardens (called game protectors) in 1935. The idea for the school came from Ross Leffler, president of the Board of Game Commissioners, who served as a commissioner for thirty years after which he was appointed Assistant Secretary of the Interior by President Dwight D. Eisenhower. My brother and I were selected for the school in 1975, and in the previous forty years, there had only been fifteen classes held, with three hundred thirty-two men graduating. So you can see why game wardens are often referred to as the thin green line, and Pennsylvania was no exception to that rule.

For John and me, it was a six-hour drive to the school in Jefferson County. In bad weather, it took us considerably longer. After turning off a dirt road north of Brockway, we cruised down a mile-long macadam lane surrounded by twenty-thousand acres of state game lands before reaching the school. Thirty men were supposed to show up on that warm, sunny day back in 1975, but one never did, deciding instead to embark on another lifelong career. Hard to believe, I thought, after everything we had gone through to be selected for the school. My brother and I had quit our jobs, both leaving wives back home (John, like many students, also had young children at home). The school term would last fifty weeks, and there were no facilities for family members to stay with us.

We arrived in a beat-up 1962 Oldsmobile that we bought for two hundred-fifty dollars, and in retrospect, it was nothing short of a miracle that the old car made the five hundred mile weekly journey to the school and back for an entire year without breaking down once. I had to sell my 1953 Wills Jeep, my pride and joy, to buy the Olds. I hated to let it go, but the jeep was geared too low, and had a maximum cruising speed of fifty-five miles per hour. It would be too slow for the long drive each week.

John and Bill standing by a patrol car on our first day.

There was an ample parking lot in front of the school. So we parked the car, grabbed our duffle bags from the trunk, and started toward the two-story white stucco building that would serve as our home away from home for the next twelve months. The school superintendent, a former Marine Corps drill sergeant, stood fence-post straight on the top step of a concrete walkway leading to the front door. He wore a straw Stetson tipped just so; his khaki shirt was ironed with enough starch to repel bullets and bore crisp, military creases that marched down the front of his shirt in line with his pocket buttons, the sleeves pressed sharp as knives. He wore forest green pants creased to a deadly edge, the sun blinding as it reflected off his gleaming black boots.

It was going to be a long year, I reckoned. A very long year indeed.

The Training School consisted of two buildings. The main building contained a kitchen and mess hall; a lounge with a large wooden table, a comfy sofa and several plush chairs; a typing room; and an office for the staff on the first floor. The upper floor held sleeping quarters and bathroom facilities for the Trainees (we were called Trainees from that day onward). Directly behind the first building was another two-story building. The first floor held a classroom and library of sorts, while the second, Spartan in design, held a single room that served as sleeping quarters for twelve men with bathroom facilities down the hall. Located roughly between these two buildings, a gigantic boulder sat along a grassy area as if dropped from the sky. It was affectionately called "The Rock," and turned out to be a place we often congregated between classes for a short cigarette break or just to hang out for a while and breathe some fresh air.

My brother and I were assigned to separate sleeping quarters: John to a room in the first building that held three narrow bunks, the other two reserved for the men who would share the room with him. I ended up in the second building with twelve trainees sharing a single room.

It was a paramilitary style training school. Instructions were explicit and to be followed precisely: Bunks to be made tight enough for a quarter to bounce off the horsehair blankets; sheets tucked into neat, hospital corners; black shoes to be polished at all times and lined under the bunk's metal edge;

nothing left lying around, clothing and all worldly belongings to be stored (crammed was more like it) neatly into narrow metal footlockers. If we failed to follow these instructions, we would get "gigged." Getting gigged meant extra work details and a memo in your file. Too many gigs and you would be terminated.

Trainees assembled on "The Rock" for a group photo.

Every morning at five a.m., the loudest, most uncivilized buzzer ever conceived by man would sound off, its ear-splitting drone reverberating through the halls sending us bolt-upright from a sound sleep. I hated that buzzer and would crawl out of my covers early each morning so that it wouldn't jar me out bed. And because I was in a room with twelve men forced to share bath facilities with only four sinks, two showers and two toilets in the adjoining room, it was always better to rise early before the others headed for the showers.

At five-twenty a.m., we would all march outside for an hour of physical training consisting of pushups, jumping jacks, and sit-ups followed by a two-mile run. Not everyone was capable of running that far, so we were allowed to walk part of the distance for the first few months. Trainees Al Scott and Mike Schmit were the exceptions. They sprinted along with the grace of gazelles, and would go for a run every afternoon if they had time. The rest of us were expected to pick up our pace each week and eventually run the entire distance nonstop in order to graduate from the school. It didn't matter how cold it got (some winter mornings it was below zero) we always did our workouts outside. When it snowed, we ran in the tire tracks left by our cook, Mrs. Adams, rather than plod through the heavy white powder. She would be at the school long before we were up.

Each week, five trainees would be assigned KP duty (Kitchen Police) and were excused from physical training to assist Mrs. Adams as she prepared meals for the staff, trainees and any guest instructors.

Men on KP having early breakfast before others arrived.

KP duties involved things like peeling potatoes and other food preparations (but not cooking), serving meals to the staff and fellow trainees, washing dishes, mopping floors, wiping tables and so on. Breakfast was at seven a.m., after which chores would be assigned to all trainees at seven-thirty when breakfast ended. The men on KP cleaned up the kitchen and the dining room while the remaining twenty-four men did everything else. The entire training facility, both buildings, had to be tackled. Floors vacuumed and mopped, bathrooms scrubbed, shelves dusted and so on. But even with all of us working as fast as we could, it was a lot to accomplish in the thirty minutes we had left before classes started at eight o'clock.

The men made short work of the bacon, eggs and sausage each morning.

While we attended the first morning class, our instructors would perform a detailed inspection of our completed chores…or at least we thought they were completed. Their goal was to find deficiencies, which they always did, sometimes while wearing white cotton gloves as they ran their hands over shelves and tabletops checking for the slightest traces of dust. When they couldn't find any surface dust, they would reach underneath the furniture and look for it there. Considering the building was sixty years old, odds were in their favor, and we almost always had to go over everything again, giving up our scheduled ten-minute break before the next class.

Our classes were varied, and we were required to study land management, wildlife management, law enforcement procedures, criminology, psychology, self-defense tactics, defensive firearms tactics, public speaking, dendrology (study of trees), ornithology (study of birds), emergency first aid, game and wildlife laws and much more. We were expected to take notes on all classes, and the notes had to be typed and were always subject to inspection. This was especially difficult for those of us who never used a typewriter before, and that included my brother and me as well as several other students. The school provided typing classes, which helped, but it took months before I evolved from the two-finger stab technique to using all of my digits on the array of keys.

Trainees could always be found typing notes between classes.

Classes ran well into the evening each day, and the daily association with fellow students provided a tremendous learning experience. We were always either in class, typing notes about a class, or studying for a test. Even during our breaks, trainees would be discussing subjects taught in class, and I would often get involved in the talks, hoping to learn something I may have missed. Our training was very intense, so much so, that a single year at the school was said to be the academic equivalent of a two-year college degree.

We were frequently subjected to unannounced written tests, and expected to maintain an eighty-percent passing score on all examinations for the entire year or face dismissal. Study time was scarce because classes often ran until nine o'clock in the evening and lights were out at ten. And because our notes had to be typed, we used a lot of our precious free time pecking away on manual typewriters at the expense of our studies. If you were slow at typing, your studies would suffer even more, and if you had a week of KP duty there was no time to study at all.

The school was unique, unlike any other in the world, I think. It was part college, part police academy and part museum, with a fifty-week training program that consisted of over fourteen hundred hours of instruction on more than a hundred different subjects taught by dozens of instructors, including game wardens and other Game Commission personnel.

We had weekends off, but we were split evenly into two units, Group A and Group B, depending on where we lived in the state, east or west of center. Consequently, and by design, half the class would be dismissed on Friday evenings at five o'clock, while the others had to stay at the school overnight and couldn't leave until their assigned chores were completed on Saturday. We were required to clean the entire school: mop floors, sweep carpets, dust all furniture, scrub bathrooms and showers, clean the kitchen, wash dishes and much more. If one trainee failed to do his job properly, we all had to wait until his assignment was completed to our superintendent's satisfaction before we would be dismissed. And though we requested permission for the entire class to get together and finish all chores on Friday evenings so we would all have a full weekend home, our superintendent wouldn't hear of it. As a result, every other weekend, either Group A (western) or Group B (eastern) would stay until Saturday afternoon while the others left at five o'clock on Friday. Because the Training School was located in western Pennsylvania, the trainees in Group B had a much longer drive home. It was a six-hour run for John and me, and a Saturday afternoon dismissal meant we wouldn't get home until eight or nine at night. And because we were required to be back at the school for lights out at ten on Sunday night, we had but eighteen hours at home before heading back to the school again.

This was difficult to handle for many trainees, especially those living in the eastern part of the state. After all, most of us had left our school days and military stints long behind us. We had careers, or at least had been working regular jobs for many years prior to attending the school, and the idea of keeping half the class for chores each Saturday seemed punitive, especially considering that we were hand-picked from over two thousand applicants—the cream of the crop, so to speak.

Superintendent Williams watches as my brother polishes his office floor.

It was particularly unfair to those with long drives back to eastern Pennsylvania each weekend. So much so, that after returning from our first weekend home, we learned that one of our classmates had quit. I overheard a trainee telling others that he'd driven the fellow home, and when he dropped him off, his wife came running out of the house with tears streaming down her cheeks. She embraced him tightly and begged him not to go back. I guess you can't blame the guy, but I often wondered if he ever regretted his decision.

Our second classmate dropped out after six weeks. Only this time it wasn't so much of a surprise, for he started complaining about the school during our breaks between classes. We were all stressed out. The school was designed that way. In fact, one day while two trainees were cleaning the superintendent's office, they overheard chatter coming from a speaker on his desk that came from some students who were cleaning the upstairs quarters. The word spread among us like wildfire: The school was bugged! The boss could hear everything we did at any given time! Man, did that give us the creeps. I suppose the motive for eavesdropping was to help cull the weak from the strong and terminate those who weren't suited for the dedicated lifestyle of a state game warden. After all, upon graduation (it was always, 'if and when you graduate,' when the superintendent addressed the class) we were expected to work days, nights, weekends and holidays during hunting season; be available to our supervisors and the public twenty-four hours per day; relocate to another county far from home if necessary; be prepared to use force, including deadly force if needed in self-defense; bring orphaned and injured wildlife to our homes for rehabilitation; investigate fatal hunting accidents; rescue lost hunters; attend all service club meetings in our assigned districts; volunteer for educational programs at service clubs, schools and churches, and keep an office in our homes with a state-owned telephone for the thousands of calls we were likely to receive each year. In other words, you were expected to be totally committed to your job and to consider it a way of life, not just another day at the office.

Classes ran from June through early October when three months of field training began, during which time each student was assigned to four three-week stints with different game wardens in various locations throughout the state. The training was continuous with only one weekend home for the entire three-month period. This was another particularly difficult time for trainees who had wives and families waiting for them at home. Fortunately, most of the married men had understanding wives who were willing to endure the disadvantage of not having a husband around while he was in training.

My first field assignment was with State Game Warden Jim Beard in Cumberland County, which is located in southcentral Pennsylvania. Jim had a spare bedroom for me in the back of the house, and I lived with him and his wife for the next three weeks. We got along fine and worked well together. Jim loved his job, and we put in a lot of sixteen-hour days. Lots of nights too. Although we made a number of arrests, we never got into any big poaching cases.

Bill performing a routine license check on a duck hunter. All was well.

There was one particular instance with Jim that I'll never forget. We were on night patrol in a rural area known for late spotlighting and poaching activity when we saw a bright yellow light arc across the sky and then quickly go out. Someone was working a spotlight in the fields behind us and they were coming our way. Poachers will often shine a field until a house or a barn appears, then arc the beam up and across the sky to avoid hitting any buildings. The last thing they want is to cast a beam into someone's home and alarm the folks inside. That could induce an irate homeowner's wrath, or worse, a heated phone call to the local game warden. Because it was after midnight, which made spotlighting for deer illegal, we intended to stop the vehicle. Jim pulled to the side of the narrow dirt road and shut off his lights, then we both climbed out of his patrol car and waited.

Through the gloom, we saw the dim outline of a vehicle as it rounded a bend in the distance and came toward us. A pickup truck with amber clearance lights dotting the roof. It was cruising slowly down the center of the road with its headlights off, guided only by the dim glow of its parking lights. Suddenly it slammed to a stop, tires digging into the gravel road. Jim glanced over at me and said, "Get ready to bail!"

As if reading Jim's mind, the truck's high beams flashed on and it came hurtling toward us at a deadly pace. There was no doubt in my mind that the truck would run us down if we didn't get out of its way. We both dove for cover at the same time, Jim to the right while I leaped to my left as the lunatic truck shot by, sideswiping Jim's vehicle parked alongside the road.

In seconds we were on our feet as the truck sped into the night. Jim and I raced toward his patrol and jumped inside. I buckled my seatbelt as he started the engine and dropped the car into gear. "Hold on!" he said, and slammed the accelerator to the floor. The sedan took off like a fighter jet rocketing down an open runway. Dust from the fleeing pickup hung in the air as we raced ahead, hoping to catch him.

"Headlights!" I shouted. "You don't have your lights on!"

Jim looked straight ahead, hands tight on the wheel. "I don't want him to see us."

I double-checked my seatbelt and took a deep breath. The pickup was nowhere in sight and Jim was flying down the narrow road at close to a hundred miles per hour guided only by the full moon. At the first curve, Jim switched on his headlights and I thanked the Lord as he slowed down. We came to a macadam crossroad and he turned right, purely guessing which way to go, and decked the accelerator once again. It was a narrow, winding, two-lane highway with many sharp curves. There was no way to make good time, but he did his best, pushing the sedan hard while braking for each bend in the road. Soon the landscape fell into a wide-ranging lowland to our left, giving us a chance to see for a considerable distance.

"There!" I shouted. "It just turned off on that side road below us." I was certain it was the same vehicle. The amber running lights a dead giveaway as the truck quickly traveled out of sight.

Jim raced ahead until he reached the road where the truck had turned and slammed his brakes, making a hard left. "They must have seen us coming," he said. "Can't even see their taillights up ahead!"

My eyes were locked on the road as Jim's sedan ate up the distance. "It's a dead end road," he said. "They're trapped!"

No sooner had he said this when we saw twin high-beams rounding a sharp bend in front of us. Above them, a telltale row of amber clearance lights. The truck was in the middle of the road, traveling toward us at breakneck speed. Once again, the driver had no intention of stopping, and had Jim not swerved into a muddy drainage ditch we would have been in a deadly head-on.

As the truck flew by, Jim eased his foot on the accelerator and moved his gearshift lever from forward to reverse and back again, using the momentum to rock his way out of the ditch. When his back wheels finally took hold, Jim turned the patrol car around and slammed the accelerator to the floor, his tires spewing thick clumps of mud behind as we raced toward the macadam crossroad we'd turned from earlier. We knew the odds of catching the fleeing truck were dim at best, and though we reached the hard road in a matter of minutes, our fugitive was long gone.

We continued to patrol the vicinity, circling a ten-square-mile area until the wee hours of the morning, hoping to see the truck, but we never did find him, and considering how crazy he'd been acting, we suspected he had at least one illegal deer in the vehicle.

It was a good lesson for me in my budding career as a game warden: sometimes, no matter how hard you try, the bad guy gets away. We had no license plate to trace and we had no idea who was driving the truck. All we could do was move forward and hope for better results the next time we encountered a poacher.

My second assignment was in Bedford County, which also lies in southcentral Pennsylvania. I was assigned to Warden Tom Barney, and lived with him and his wife at their home for another three weeks. This was an entirely different environment from Game Warden Beard's district. Deer poaching was rampant here. At dusk we could hear distant gunfire every evening. Some nights it sounded like a war zone there was so much shooting. We'd go on night patrol frequently but never caught any poachers during my stay with Tom. But with a territory encompassing almost four hundred square miles and only one patrol car, we couldn't be everywhere at once and the poachers had a huge advantage, as they always do everywhere. I'll never forget the time we drove into the village of Defiance and watched grown men running helter-skelter into their homes at the sight of our patrol car. I'll never forget the time we were on patrol and I saw a sign in an open pasture that read, *night shooters, goats in field*. A warning—or request, I suppose would be more accurate—for poachers not to shoot one of the farmer's goats in mistake for a deer. But of all the incidents during my stay with Tom Barney, the one I remember most was when I was called into regional headquarters to meet with an FBI agent who wanted information about a death list they found belonging to a woman who had just been arrested for attempting to assassinate the president of the United States.

It was a warm summer day in September 1975 when Lynette Alice "Squeaky" Fromme went to Capital Park in Sacramento to plead with President Ford about the proposed destruction of California redwood trees, armed with a .45 caliber handgun. Fortunately, a Secret Service agent restrained her before anyone was injured. She refused to cooperate in her own defense at her trial and was eventually convicted of attempting to assassinate the president and sentenced to life in prison. She later told the press that she "came to get life. Not just my life but clean air, healthy water, and respect for creatures and creation."

Ironic, considering she was a known associate of convicted murderer Charles Manson, a criminal cult leader who formed the Manson Family, a desert commune consisting primarily of female followers who were habitual drug users radicalized by Manson's teachings and attracted by a hippie culture and the idea of communal living. Manson's followers committed a series of nine murders at four locations in July and August 1969. In 1971, he was convicted of first-degree murder and conspiracy to commit murder for the deaths of seven people, all of which members of the group carried out at his instruction. Manson was also convicted of first-degree murder for two other deaths.

When the FBI searched Fromme's apartment, they discovered a list of names that targeted various people for assassination. My wife and I were on that list, which is why I was sitting in front of an FBI agent who was asking me why.

"You're asking *me!*" I said. "You're the FBI. Why don't *you* tell *me*?"

I was shocked. I had no idea how or why my wife and I ended up on a death list belonging to someone who just tried to murder our president. A million thoughts flooded my mind. Most of them bad. My wife lived at home alone. I was hundreds of miles away. How could I protect her? What if someone was at the house now, waiting for her to come home from work? What if the Game Commission suspected that I was tied into the Manson Family? Would they kick me out of the school? Maybe it was time to leave, anyway, I thought. How could I stay hundreds of miles away when my wife might be in danger? I asked the regional supervisor if I could take a couple days off to go home. He agreed, so I left right away.

I drove directly home. Nonstop. Five hours. It was after dark when I arrived, and Maryann was just getting home from work. I explained what I had learned from the FBI and had her wait outside while I went in and searched the house. I checked the basement first, then went upstairs and inspected every room. Later that night we talked. Maryann did not want me to quit the training school. It meant too much to me, and she knew I'd forever regret leaving. She was scared but refused to show it. And she was dead serious about my staying at the school. Although she wasn't comfortable around guns, Maryann knew how to shoot and told me she started keeping a revolver in a dresser next to the bed for protection.

"Since when," I asked.

"I didn't want to tell you while you were away, but someone broke into the house and stole some things."

"What things?" I said. I was stunned to hear of it.

"Some of my jewelry and some money I had left on the kitchen table. Nothing expensive."

"How did they get in?"

"They found a window that wasn't locked, forced it open and crawled in. I reported it to the police. They're investigating."

"This is terrible!" I said. "Death lists, burglars, what's next?"

The following morning, after breakfast, I stepped out on our second-story balcony to enjoy a view of the countryside and my heart stopped. A heavy, ten-foot wooden ladder I had built from two-by-four lumber and left lying alongside the house was propped against the balcony. For all I knew, it could have been standing there for days, and probably was. Someone had either tried to get into the house by climbing the ladder and entering the glass sliding door or had been secretly standing on the rungs with their head just above the floor of the balcony, watching.

I didn't think it was anyone connected to Lynette Fromme; she was in prison, and anyone associated with her had to suspect that the death list had been discovered and potential victims warned. I strongly suspected that the ladder had been placed by a neighbor who lived within walking distance of my house.

The next day, my suspicions were confirmed. It was after dark, and my wife's sister, Lorraine, and her husband, Joe, were just pulling into their driveway. They lived next door to us, and Joe happened to look over toward our house when he spotted the silhouette of a man standing by our bedroom window as he peered inside. Joe jumped out of his car and came charging after him. But the pervert heard him coming and took off. He had a good head start and was able to disappear into the night before Joe could catch him. My brother-in-law is a big man. Had he caught the wierdo, I can assure you it would have been the last time he ever peeked into a window again.

The combination of my wife being on some lunatic's death list and living alone with thieves lurking about while some creep was peeping into our windows was too much to bear. I disassembled the ladder piece by piece, put up additional spotlights outside, and alerted the police along with Game Warden Lockett and his deputies. One particular deputy owned several German shepherd dogs and stopped by with a female named Rosie later that day, offering to loan her to us while I was away at the training school. We readily accepted his offer and breathed a collective sigh of relief. Rosie took to Maryann immediately and always stayed by her side. Whenever she returned from work or shopping, she would give Rosie a warm greeting and say, "Go check the house!" Rosie would immediately turn and look through every room, even nosing open closet doors that weren't closed tightly, ensuring my wife that everything was safe. Whenever anyone came to the door, Rosie would stand next to Maryann and growl at them. She was a great protector and we both loved her very much.

I returned to Bedford County and spent two more weeks patrolling with Game Warden Barney before heading home for a scheduled weekend off prior to my next field assignment. Rosie accepted me as part of her adopted family whenever I came home, but she wouldn't let anyone else into the house, including Maryann's relatives unless she calmly assured Rosie that it was okay.

I continued to wonder how my wife and I ended up on an assassination list kept by someone we had never met or knew about until her incident with President Ford, which made national news. The FBI, in their infinite wisdom, chose not to disclose this information to me, and it wasn't until twenty years later that I found out when I happened to read *Illusions of Animal Rights* by Russ Carman and discovered that he and his wife were on the same death list. I knew Russ personally; he and I both served as officers in the Pennsylvania Trappers Association (PTA), and I suspected that that had something to do with it. I telephoned him immediately and found my suspicions were confirmed, for Russ told me that the president, vice president, secretary and treasurer of the PTA were all on the list. As it turned out, the alleged offense warranting death was that we were trappers.

My third and fourth assignments were in northeastern Pennsylvania during big game season with three weeks in Lackawanna County followed by three weeks in Wayne County. Both officers arranged for me to stay in their homes rather than live in an apartment someplace. I was fine with the arrangement. Although it's always a bit uncomfortable living with a new family for the first time, the upside is that you get a firsthand glimpse of what it's like to live the life of a state game warden and see how it impacts family life (you were right there when friction developed between husband and wife or parents and children…and we know it always does at some point, especially when you're working day and night during hunting season).

State Game Warden Chet Cinamella was my mentor during my assignment in Lackawanna County. Part of his district included the city of Scranton (the sixth largest city in the commonwealth with a population of seventy-seven thousand), a place we tried to stay away from as much as possible. Actually, it wasn't too difficult to do, as most of Lackawanna County was rural and heavily forested. Hunting pressure was heavy, too, due to the substantial human population there (close to a quarter million people). Even so, we didn't get into any big deer poaching cases and spent most of our patrol days handling minor game law infractions. But sometimes the most trivial violation can turn deadly in a matter of seconds. Especially when you least expect it.

We were on routine patrol in a mountainous and heavily forested area of northern Lackawanna County when Chet turned down a narrow country road sprinkled with deer camps. Buck season was in full swing (two weeks of buck season followed by two days of doe season back in those days) and the camps were crammed with empty pickup trucks and automobiles that belonged to hunters putting on drives or posted by their favorite stand. We didn't want to venture into the woods and risk ruining someone's hunt, so we continued to drive along the mountain road intending to check any deer that we saw hanging at a camp. Halfway down the road, we came across a gray-haired hunter walking toward us carrying a rifle. He was in his late sixties, and as soon as he spotted our patrol car he did a one-eighty, slung the rifle over his shoulder, and walked hurriedly back toward his cabin thirty yards away. He didn't have a hunting license pinned to his back, so Chet immediately pulled over and parked. We both jumped out and started toward the hunter as Chet called for him to hold up, but he continued walking at a brisk pace, managing to keep several yards between us. As we approached the cabin, we could see a dead deer lying off to the side. When he reached the deer, the hunter pulled a hunting license from his coat pocket and threw it on top of animal—an untagged spike buck—before quickly ducking into the cabin.

Chet called for him to come back outside but he refused, so we pocketed his license, and started dragging the deer back toward our patrol car. We were halfway to the car, when the man came running out of the cabin followed by five others—all with rifles.

"Bring back my deer!" he hollered. "You got no right!"

We stopped and faced him. His followers, younger than he, stood directly behind him when he reached us, and although their barrels were pointed skyward, it was an unnerving situation.

"Give me back my deer!" he barked. There was a heavy revolver holstered at his side.

"We're confiscating it," Chet told him. "It's untagged."

"Untagged!" he scoffed. "You got my license. I saw you pick it up. My tag is right there!"

Chet remained cool. The old man was obviously playing dumb. He knew that his tag had to be detached from the license and filled out to be legal.

"You'll be getting a citation in the mail," said Chet. "The fine is twenty-five dollars."

The old man's eyes narrowed into slits, his lips drawing into a scowl of contempt. "I'm going to shoot you right here!" he roared, reaching for his gun.

In those days we wore bulky winter coats that fell to our hips. They weren't designed for law enforcement and had no side-zipper for a quick gun extraction. To make matters worse, the Game Commission's issue gun was a .38 caliber revolver with a two-inch barrel. We were at point-blank range. There was no way either of us could hoist up our heavy coats and retrieve a handgun before the old man shot both of us. And even if we could, the five armed men standing by him, whom I assumed were family, clearly had us outgunned. All of this flashed through my mind in a millisecond as his right hand fell toward his weapon. Knowing I had to stop him before he drew his gun, I lunged at him, my hands pushing his revolver back into the holster as my right shoulder knocked him to the ground. Tripping over his feet as he went down, I lost balance and fell down right next to him. Smooth operator I wasn't.

With his gun safely in my hands, I got to my feet and backed away from the group. Two men bent over and quickly helped him up. Had they not been standing directly behind him to break his fall, he likely would have been injured. As it turned out, he was merely humiliated.

He pointed a crooked finger at my face. "YOU SON OF A—"

But he was cut off. "*Pops!*" one of the men shouted. "These guys are cops! You can't kill them just because they took your deer! The woods are full of deer. Go shoot another one."

The old man shook himself off and glared hatefully at me as I stuffed his gun into the small of my back. "You don't know who you're messing with son," he warned. Then he turned suddenly and stormed back into the cabin, his hands clenched into tight fists.

Chet signaled for me to let him walk away. He was right. The situation was tense enough, and there was no sense making the matter any worse by going after him. Besides, we had his hunting license, so it would be a simple matter to use the information to file citations against him later.

The one who called him Pops offered us a lame smile. "He wasn't gonna shoot you," he said. "Pops just lost his temper, that's all." He was a barrel-chested man with chestnut brown eyes and skin the color of bronze. He had a Roman nose and a thick, protruding chin. His lips were like carved granite and set in a perpetual scowl.

"Didn't look that way to us," said Chet.

"No. Really," the man insisted, "he was just blowing off steam, that's all."

"Interference with an officer carries a heavy penalty," said Chet. "It could have been a simple twenty-five dollar fine, now it'll be five hundred."

The man shrugged. "He can afford it. When do we get his gun back?"

"After he pays his fine. No sooner."

"That gun is very special to my father."

"We'll be sure to take good care of it."

"Can we pay you now?"

Said Chet, "Your father can sign a field receipt and plead guilty if he wants, but you can't do it for him." (In those days, most fines were settled by paying cash and signing a field acknowledgement of guilt. The Game Commission ceased using this method in the mid-1980s.).

He turned to one of the men. "Cheech," he said, "tell Pops he can't get his gun back unless he pleads guilty and pays five hundred bucks. Tell him I've got the cash; all he has to do is sign a piece of paper."

Cheech was a dopy looking man with slick black hair and heavily lidded eyes that gave the impression he just woke up. "Sure Nicky," he said. Then he ran down to the cabin and slipped inside. After several minutes, Cheech opened the front door and called out to us. "Pops said he would sign, but only for Warden Cinamella, not the wise guy that attacked him."

Chet stifled a laugh and rolled his eyes at me. Then he called back to Cheech saying he'd be right over. Chet walked over to his patrol car and grabbed a metal citation pad from the back seat. Inside was an assortment of blank field acknowledgements and citations. "Be right back," he told me.

While Chet was inside with the old man, Nicky looked at the patch on my coat sleeve and frowned. "Trainee, huh," he remarked. "Is that like a deputy or something?"

I hated that we had to wear uniform patches with *Trainee* printed on them. "Yes," I said. "I've been a deputy game warden for over a year, but I'm in training for a full time position right now."

Nicky nodded understandingly. "You got guts," he said. "I like that." He turned to the others. "He's a brave man, tackling Pops like that. Huh?"

"Yeah, real brave, Nicky," someone said. The others stared at me with predatory eyes.

In truth, I was pretty scared the whole time. My reaction was impulsive. It was either dive for the gun or risk getting shot. Chet couldn't have gotten to him in time. The confiscated deer was lying on the ground next to us and Chet was standing on the opposite side. I didn't have to hurdle the carcass to reach the old man like he would have. Only a few feet had separated us. So I reacted. Bravery had nothing to do with it.

It was clear that Nicky was mocking me. I didn't like Nicky. I thought about demanding to see his hunting license, but something told me that I should let things simmer down. Count my blessings, so I didn't.

Rather than stand there and wait for more sarcasm from Nicky, I decided to load the deer on Chet's big game rack. It would give me a chance to get away from what I considered to be a bunch of thugs. I grabbed the deer by a front leg and started dragging it over to our patrol car when Nicky called out to me. "Where you going with Pop's deer?"

"I don't know whose deer it is," I shot back. "It's not tagged." I instantly regretted my remark, knowing it would only serve to set him off.

"So, you think I'm a liar, huh?" he said, his question sounding more like a threat. "I told you it's Pop's deer."

I don't know what would have happened had Chet not come walking out the cabin door at that moment. Cheech was two steps behind him. "Bill!" called Chet. "You can leave the deer. I have his tag filled out."

Nicky turned to Chet when he got close. "Thank you, officer," he said. "Maybe you should teach your trainee some manners."

"Maybe you should come up with the five hundred for your father's fine," remarked Chet. He showed Nicky the signed field acknowledgement of guilt indicating his father had pled guilty to interfering with an officer in the performance of his duty.

Nicky reached deep into his pants pocket and pulled out a wad of cash that must have been four inches thick. He peeled off five hundred-dollar bills and handed them to Chet, counting them off one by one. Chet pocketed the cash and gave Nicky a copy of the signed field receipt while Cheech attached Pops big game tag to the deer's ear.

"Pop's gun?" said Nicky, eyeing me cautiously.

I pulled it from behind my back, flipped open the cylinder and emptied six .357 Magnum rounds into my opposite hand.

Grasping the gun by the barrel, I handed it to Nicky, grip first, then dumped the six cartridges into his other hand.

"Thank you, gentlemen," he said. "Now get back out there and look for some *real* poachers."

Chet smiled sarcastically and motioned for me to follow him back to his car. I was glad to oblige.

The old man isn't mad at you anymore," he said as he steered off the narrow mountain road onto a highway. Thirty minutes of silence had preceded his comment. My mind still focused on our run-in with the men at the camp.

"Excuse me," I said.

Chet glanced at me then back to the road. "I said Vito isn't mad at you anymore."

"Am I supposed to care?"

"Maybe. Ever hear of the Bonomo crime family?"

"Yeah," I said. "They operate out of New York city, right?"

Chet nodded while looking straight ahead. "Know how far that is from us?"

"Not exactly."

"A two-hour drive."

"Why are you telling me this?"

The old man is Vito Bonomo. Nicky—real name Nicolo—is one of his sons."

I felt the hairs on the back of my neck stiffen. "Are you saying these guys are the Mafia?"

"It's not that *I'm* saying it…the news media has been talking about them for years. Vito is supposed to be one of the bosses out of New York."

"So what's he gonna do, put a contract out on me?" I scoffed.

"You never know."

I looked at Chet and waited for a laugh, thinking it was all a joke. When it didn't come, I said, "You're serious, aren't you?"

He shrugged. "Vito was embarrassed that you knocked him down. He started badmouthing you as soon as I walked in the door. Wanted to know your name. Where you live. Stuff like that."

I said, "What did he expect me to do, say please don't shoot us?"

"Exactly. It's always the same with these guys. Nothing is ever their fault; it's always ours or somebody else's."

"What did you say to him?"

"I said you were a good man and that somebody already had a contract out on you and your wife, and that the FBI was involved. That stopped him cold. He was all ears." With that, Chet turned into the parking lot of a local diner and stopped. "Hungry?" he said.

It was mid-day and I was starved. "Yes," I said, "but what else did he say?"

"He said he knew about Squeaky Fromme, of course. Who doesn't? Knew about Charles Manson, too. Said he was a punk. He wanted to know why you were on, what he called, a 'hit list,' and I told him you never met Fromme or any of the Manson followers before and had no idea, but you and your wife were on a death list discovered in her apartment. He thought for a moment and then said maybe you did something to deserve it, but not your wife. 'Nobody puts a contract out on a man's wife,' he said. Then he told me to fill out my citations so he could eat his lunch in peace. When he was done signing, he slid the papers across the table to me. 'Now get outta here,' he said. 'And tell your deputy he should go home and look after his wife.'"

"He said that?"

"Yep."

"That was actually pretty decent of him."

"Yeah, it was," agreed Chet. "After lunch you've got two days off at home."

"The Game Commission won't care?" I asked in surprise.

"Let me worry about that. Now let's go eat."

My next field assignment was in northern Wayne County with State Game Warden Fred Weigelt. He was fun to be with and had a great sense of humor. With over twenty-five years of service, Fred was the oldest and most experienced officer of my four field assignments. He was, understandably, the most laidback too. And it was a welcome relief, as the seemingly endless tour of sixteen-hour days was starting to wear me down. Don't get me wrong. It's not like we sat around playing cards all day. Fred was a dedicated officer and we worked long hours. After all, buck season was still open, with a two-day doe season scheduled toward the end of my stay. And Wayne County had plenty of pressure, with scores of hunters coming from as far away as Philadelphia, New York and New Jersey.

Of all the places in Pennsylvania to work as a game warden, Wayne County was at the top of my list. I'd done some beaver trapping there years earlier and came to love the rolling hills and broad valleys that make up most of the landscape. There are a lot of lakes and streams in the county as well, which affords some of the best trapping territory to be found anywhere. The deer population was more than ample for all the hunting pressure we had, but surprisingly, we never got into any big poaching cases while I was there. In fact, we made just a handful of arrests during my entire stay.

One case that comes to mind happened on the last day of buck season when Fred received a tip regarding baiting in the northern part of his district. It was on private property, and we drove out there the following day to check it out. We had a few inches of snow on the ground, and when we reached the property, the person who had called was standing along the road waiting for us. He was eager to get started. "I hope they haven't left already," he said anxiously. "They've been here since yesterday."

He offered us a hand and we shook. In his mid-forties, he was tall with a gaunt face and three days of heavy stubble on his cheeks. "Is this your property?" asked Fred.

"No, it's my neighbor's. He lives in New Jersey and doesn't come around much. He lets me hunt here as long as I watch the property for him."

"Do you know who's back there?"

"No, but there's two of them. Neither of these guys is wearing orange and there was a bunch of apples scattered in the snow between them. They're posted about fifty yards apart. When I saw them, I just kept walking like I didn't notice the bait. They didn't say a word to me and I didn't say anything to them, either." With that, he started walking into the field and motioned for us to follow. "We better get going," he said. "I'd hate to see them kill that ten-pointer I've been after."

We continued across the meadow, walking continuously downhill toward a large wooded area when our informant suddenly stopped. "Look! Somebody's down there."

A bearded man wearing a camouflage jacket and hat was walking through the trees a hundred yards ahead. We picked up our pace as Fred called out to him. "State officer! Stop where you are!"

He obeyed immediately, shouldering his rifle, he turned toward us and stuffed both hands in his pockets as we approached. Fred took his rifle and handed it to me. Next he inspected his hunting license as our informant stood silently by.

After a moment, Fred looked at him with a raised brow. "Whose license is this?"

"It's mine."

"So your first name is Linda?"

The hunter looked at Fred with feigned surprise. "Whoops!" he said. "I must have taken my wife's license by mistake!"

Fred pocketed his license and shook his head. "I'll tell you what I think," he said. "You killed your buck already and now you're using your wife's license to kill another one."

"No way! Honest, officer. I grabbed it off the kitchen table by mistake. Mine was right next to hers."

Fred knew there was no way to prove he was right, but there was a game law fine on the books for anyone hunting with another's license, and he intended to use it.

"Where were you going when we stopped you?" asked Fred. "You looked like you were in a hurry."

"I was ready to go home when I realized I'd forgotten my thermos," he said. "It's back in the woods. A long walk from here, too."

"Is that where you were hunting earlier?"

"Yeah."

"Were you using apples for bait?"

He paused in surprise, then quickly regained himself. "Not me! But I did see someone hunting over some apples earlier today."

"He's lying, officer!" blurted our informant. "It was him. I'm sure of it."

The bearded man whipped his head around and stared at our informant. Then, slowly, his face began to change as he realized he was the same person who had walked past him an hour before. The man let out a long sigh of regret and nodded solemnly. "He's right," he said to Fred. "I was hunting with apples. I'm sorry I did it."

"Where is the person you were hunting with?" asked Fred. "We know there were two of you."

"That would be my uncle. He's back at the car, waiting for me."

"Let's take a walk," said Fred. "I want you to show us where you were hunting."

We followed him back into the woods until we came to a clearing with several dozen apples spread around. After taking photographs of the bait, we proceeded out of the woods and followed our poacher through the snow back to his car. His uncle sat stiffly inside the vehicle, watching as we approached. After questioning him for a short time, he admitted that he'd been hunting deer in the same baited woodlot with his nephew earlier that day.

Both men settled on field acknowledgments of guilt and paid their fines in cash. The bearded man was fined for using a borrowed license and for hunting over bait. The other, for hunting over bait with no additional charges. The penalty for using bait was twenty-five dollars in those days. Had they killed a deer, it would have been much higher.

Fred Weigelt and I continued patrolling the county for the remainder of the day, and though we came across a number of deer hunters, we found no additional violations, and headed back to Fred's house after dark. Buck season had officially ended at sunset. Doe season would begin on Monday, just thirty-six hours later.

Back then, there was a two day statewide doe season held on the Monday and Tuesday following the last day of buck season. But there was always the chance of a one-day extension if the kill was low due to bad weather or some other phenomenon like poor hunter turnout or just plain bad luck in the woods. We had ten days off for Christmas once our field training was over. It was scheduled to begin the day after doe season ended, and I remember sitting in Fred Weigelt's patrol car as we cruised through some remote part of his district, waiting for the announcement that would come over his radio advising all game wardens about the extension. We were both ready for a break from the long hours of patrol and all the other tasks that accompanied hunting season. But I was especially eager to see it come to an end. Field training had been exhausting. I suspect partially because the game wardens we were assigned to felt obligated to show us as much as possible while we were with them. But working day and night for three months, knowing I was being evaluated on everything I did...or didn't do, had taken its toll. So when Fred Weigelt's radio began to crackle at three o'clock on Tuesday afternoon, signifying a statewide announcement from the front office in Harrisburg, my heart began to pound.

"*Harrisburg to all Division Headquarters! There will be NO extension of the statewide antlerless deer season. The season ends at sunset today.*"

Fred and I exchanged smiles of relief. "Ready to go home?" he asked.

"Yes," I said.

He glanced at his watch. "Slow day today. How 'bout we head back a little early so you can get packed."

"I'd like that," I said.

I had lived with Fred and his wife for three weeks. They were gracious hosts, and I greatly enjoyed their company. Still, it was good to go home.

We were back at the Training School right after Christmas. Twelve inches of snow covered the ground under a cold gray sky, and most of our classes were pretty boring, mainly because most of our instructors were pretty boring. So much so, that I found myself falling asleep at times. But at least I made it through field training. Things could have been worse. Two of our classmates never returned. They flunked out. We were now down to twenty-five men from the original thirty, and the ominous words of our superintendent floated in my head like a bad dream:

If and when you graduate. If and when you graduate. If and when you grad...

"TRAINEE!"

I jerked my head up. It was Jim Williams, our superintendent. He was standing at the doorway of the classroom, hands on his hips, glaring at me. The room became so quiet you could hear a fly sail into a wall. I blinked repeatedly as all heads turned my way, their faces expressing genuine sympathy.

I had fallen asleep while a land management officer stood at the podium speaking in a dull monotone about clearcutting state game lands and other wearisome tasks that were part of his daily life. The subject was incredibly boring to me. I had no interest in land management. All I wanted to do was catch poachers. Be a real game warden. Forty minutes into the class, I could barely keep my eyes open, eventually falling into a state of suspended consciousness with my elbow on the desktop while propping my head with a fist.

"Mrs. Adams needs help peeling potatoes!" barked Williams. "Head over to the kitchen and give her a hand."

Humiliated (and a bit shaken I have to admit), I rose from my desk and reported directly to the kitchen. Mrs. Adams was bent over the sink cleaning a large pot and smiled at me when

I walked in. She knew I was being punished, but pretended she didn't. "Ah!" she said cheerily. "Aren't you a godsend. I'm getting way behind for dinner and I'm sure the men will be hungry. Hope you don't mind peeling for me."

There was a long stainless steel table behind her with a large pile of fist-sized potatoes in the center. "Glad to help," I said.

She nodded appreciatively and I walked by her and got to work before Mr. Williams came by to check on me.

Mrs. Adams

Peeling potatoes was more interesting than the class had been, so I actually didn't mind. There were fifty of them, and it gave me time to think as I shaved their rough brown skins into an open sink. One thing that played on my mind often was the mystery surrounding why two of our classmates hadn't come back from field training. The fact that we were never told why—not even a hint about what they did wrong—troubled many of us. I couldn't help but think it was being done by design—the not telling, I mean. More psychological drama from our tough-as-nails superintendent, so we could spend our days wondering if we'd be next to get axed.

If and when you graduate...

Of the two, I had always suspected one might not make it back. He was highly intelligent, but kind of a creampuff: a soft and pudgy guy who was on the lazy side and seemed more fitted for a nine-to-five office job...like a banker or something. Why the other classmate didn't come back was perplexing. He was a smart guy. Athletic and good-natured. He got along with everyone and seemed to love the idea of being a game warden. And the fact that he was let go made everyone uneasy for the remainder of the year. Halfway through the potatoes, I put the matter to rest, certain that we would never know the answer anyway.

When I finished peeling, it was time for the regular KP guys to come in and help prepare the evening meal. I stayed with them, setting cups and plates on the long wooden table in the mess hall while the others kept busy in the kitchen with Mrs. Adams. She made the best lemon meringue pie, and it was on the menu tonight. Hooray!

We spent a lot of time studying game laws at the school. Aside from Superintendent Williams and his assistant Mr. Furry, both active and retired field officers were invited to teach classes. Some of these men were well known to us long before they arrived. Legends in their own time, achieving their mythical status from the number of arrests they averaged each year and the rugged individualism they displayed. It was common for some of them to be introduced to the class with their arrest records following their names: "This is District Game Protector (our title in those days) Aaron Smith. He averages over a hundred prosecutions each year."

And it was these men who became instant heroes to me. It wasn't the number of prosecutions they made (although that held great significance), as much as their dogged work ethic. The Game Commission estimated that over a million hunters beat the bushes in Pennsylvania each year, with most of them afield during the statewide buck and doe seasons. In those days we had 124 full-time game wardens holding the line against the vast army of hunters saturating the state. While most hunters are honest people, we had a percentage of outlaws too, and they were scattered throughout forty-five thousand square miles of real estate encompassing Pennsylvania. It was only the most dedicated men, working day and night, who could average a hundred or more prosecutions each year. And I wanted to be just like them.

Some of the classes, like timber stand improvement in the dead of winter, seemed more like a test of will than anything educational. The idea was to open a canopy in the forest to provide better habitat for deer and other game species. Many of us were handed axes to complete the job. Thinking back, I can't remember if they needed sharpening or if the trees were frozen or both, but I do remember most of our axes bouncing back at us when they hit a tree.

We did tree pruning in winter too. Some of the men really loved it and climbed high up in the branches with their pruning shears, while most of us stayed on the ground and cut what we could reach from there.

Firearms training was scheduled regularly. I took it very serious, as did everyone else, knowing your ability with a gun might save your life or someone else's one day. We practiced every week, rain or shine. Much of our handgun training involved shooting at bullseye targets with Colt revolvers that had six-inch barrels. We also shot with Smith & Wesson snub nose .38 Specials and shotguns. The Game Commission had a statewide shooting competition each year and our training put a lot of emphasis on accuracy and precision. The objective being who could score the most points by hitting the center bullseye. We also had a lot of Practical Police Course training using human silhouette targets.

Trainees shooting the Practical Police Course

Our self-defense classes were held in an old barn that stood a hundred yards from the school. The barn was our gym of sorts. There was a steel pole secured across two wooden posts for pull-ups, a barbell with an assortment of rusting iron plates, and a half-dozen heavy dumbbells. We also had several folding mats for protection from hard falls during self-defense training. The barn wasn't heated, but it was all we had, and my brother and I used to go there to lift weights whenever we had free time.

Self-defense training was one of my favorite classes. Our instructor was Barry Warner, a game warden from Bedford County. Barry was a powerful, barrel-chested man who had been an undefeated wrestler when he was in the Navy. He also held a black belt in judo. He was a man of few words, which made his presence all the more intimidating, not to mention the fact that his uniform shirts had an eighteen-inch neck size.

John Shutter holding Al Scott in a bear hug while Warner looks on

We had a number of training scenarios provided by Barry Warner, but one of my favorites was the "bad guy" against the game wardens. We had one student acting as the outlaw while two of us tried to take him down and secure him in handcuffs. The "bad guy" was required to do his best not to let us make the arrest. It was a real wakeup call when we realized how difficult it was to subdue someone who didn't want to be taken down, although I doubt Warner would have had much trouble. I'll never forget the time he told me to put him in a bear hug. It was all I could do to stretch my arms around his huge ribcage, which felt solid as a truck tire, when he thrust out his chest and knocked me back several feet.

The class I dreaded the most was public speaking. I was on the quiet side all my life. I never associated with a lot of people in school or in work and mostly kept to myself. My closest friends were my twin brother and my wife. So when it was time to stand up in front of the class and speak, I got nervous. My heart would start pounding and my chest would tighten. Sometimes I'd open my mouth to speak and nothing would come out. I'd stand there like a fish gulping for air, feeling like a fool. But the superintendent's words, *if and when you graduate*, would come back to haunt me, and I'd take a deep breath, keep my eyes focused on the back of the room rather than my classmates blank stares, and will myself the resolve to get through it. There was no doubt in my mind that if the superintendent felt that I couldn't speak in front of large groups he would not allow me to graduate from the Training School.

The Wasserman brothers. Who's who?

Perhaps that is why he decided that my brother and I should teach some classes on fur trapping for the Trainees. We were the only trappers in the class, and most of the students had no idea how trapping actually worked, or even how to set a trap for that matter. How could they be effective enforcement officers if they didn't know where to look for trapping violations the Superintendent reasoned. In retrospect, I think it was the trapping classes we taught that got me over the hump with my fear of public speaking. I loved talking about traps and trapping, and once I got started, it was difficult to stop.

But to my surprise, a few of the students were opposed to trapping and thought it was unnecessarily cruel, and that traps could chop an animals foot off. Some challenged me on the subject, daring me to place my hand in a steel-jawed trap to see how it felt. I accepted the dare and stuck my hand into the open jaws of a double coil-spring fox trap. Yes, it hurt a little, but it didn't break any bones as some suggested—didn't even break my skin. I reminded them that there is a big difference between humans and animals. If that weren't true, animals would need boots to protect their feet, just as we do, I told them. On the contrary, animals can run on rocks, snow, ice and other rough surfaces without any sign of discomfort.

John joined me by telling the class that traps don't chop the feet off animals, explaining that conscientious trappers do everything in their power to prevent excessive stress to an animal's foot by using properly sized traps. Traps are not torture devices, he added, they're merely holding devices, and said that we had come across animals that were sound asleep in our traps on some days. This is because foothold traps apply pressure to an animal's foot, which causes numbness by decreasing circulation, thereby eliminating physical pain.

Most of the class understood, but there were a few who remained unconvinced, and from that day forward, John and I were nicknamed The Bludgeon Brothers. We got a good chuckle out of it—anything to relieve stress at the school, I suppose. Nicknames helped do that by giving students a sense of comradery. After all, we were in it together and were constantly pulling for each other. But while many of us had nicknames like *Bulldog, Dutch, Bones, Dad* and others, ours seemed to denote a degree of disparagement.

Some folks believe in Karma (what goes around comes around), and I've found there's often a degree of truth in the old saying. For instance, several days after defending trapping in front of the class and receiving our new nicknames, a groundhog started chewing holes in the radiator hoses of cars parked at the school. To make matters worse, students didn't find out until they were on their way home for the weekend and ended up stuck along the highway with an overheated engine. The first car to be harmed belonged to a student who was strongly opposed to trapping (Karma), but the ill-behaved groundhog struck fear in the hearts of every Trainee, for nobody knew whose car would be next or where the critter was coming from. Shooting it would be next to impossible, because we were all too busy with classes and couldn't spare the time to wait around for it to show up. But one day a classmate saw the chisel-toothed vandal run from under a parked car and duck into a culvert pipe under the macadam parking lot. When he told the class what he'd seen, John and I volunteered to set a trap for the groundhog and became instant heroes when we caught the varmint that very afternoon. Needless to say, attitudes about trapping improved considerably, especially among those who'd been in doubt a few days earlier.

When April finally arrived, I started counting the days until our June graduation. Many of us were on edge from the continual inspections that characterize a paramilitary lifestyle. It never let up, and we were under constant evaluation in everything we did. This affected some more than others, but I think those with a military background accepted the daily rigor better than most. Stress affects different people in different ways, and it sure took its toll on me, for I began passing small amounts of blood during my visits to the lavatory. My guts were always churning inside and I felt tired all the time. One day I told the superintendent that I wasn't feeling well and he sent me to a doctor in Brockway. The doctor did a basic physical examination but didn't do any bloodwork or lab tests of any kind. He diagnosed my condition as a symptom of anxiety from life at the school and told me not to say anything about it or they would kick me out. I believed him and kept my mouth shut.

What I didn't know at the time was that I had the beginning stages of ulcerative colitis, a chronic inflammatory bowel disease that causes inflammation and ulcers in the digestive track. I won't get into all of the symptoms, but it does cause severe fatigue, abdominal pain, blood loss and severe cramping. Most people have moderate ulcerative colitis, but I wasn't most people, and it had a dramatic effect on my health. I often told my wife that I wouldn't wish it on my worst enemy. These symptoms followed me all through the Training School but I never let anyone know. *If and when you graduate* echoed in the deep recesses of my mind, so my plight was a secret told only to my brother and my wife. The disease plagued me for the next twenty years until I finally had corrective surgery at the Cleveland Clinic in Ohio.

Along with the mild spring weather came Land Management assignments, Game Farm assignments (where ring-necked pheasants were raised) and the state tour.

Trainees visit Pymatuning State Park in Crawford County

In reverse: the state tour was just that, a tour of the state, along with the six division offices (now called regional offices) and the Harrisburg headquarters. It was interesting to visit Commission owned game lands in every corner of the state and see how unique some of these properties were compared to other areas in Pennsylvania. One thing I'll never forget was the time we made a stop for gasoline and a classmate mistakenly filled the state car with diesel fuel instead of regular gas. He didn't get too far afterwards, maybe a mile or so when the engine conked out. Embarrassing for him and costly for the state, but mistakes happen and he wasn't reprimanded for his error...well, maybe a little.

The Game Farm assignment was nothing more than a week of free farm labor for the Game Commission. There were four pheasant farms at the time, two in the western half of the state and two in the east. We were split into four groups with each group of Trainees assigned to a specific Game Farm. The highlight of my week was to see who could run the fastest with a wheelbarrow full of birdseed. I understood the educational aspect of learning how the Game Farm worked, but we could have done it in a single day without losing one scintilla of the wisdom necessary to be a state game warden.

The Land Management assignment was actually fun. Trainees were split into pairs and assigned to different Land Managers throughout the state. I was paired with Al Scott. Back at the Training School, Scottie and I used to go out to the barn and practice boxing when we had free time. The first time we boxed, Scottie handed me protective leather headgear to wear and when I asked where his protection was, he smiled and said that I was wearing it! I thought, okay, if he didn't mind getting hit, I'd just go easy on him. Thing is, Scottie was training for his first professional bout when he was selected for the Training School, and I soon discovered why he offered me his headgear. When I tried to hit him, he would simply shift his head right or left, dodging my punch. Made it look easy, too. Then he would jab me square in the forehead (protected by headgear) so fast I'd never see it coming. I never hit him once in all the times we practiced, but he must have tagged me a hundred times.

Scottie and I were assigned to Will Peoples in Wayne County for our Land Management assignment. I liked Will Peoples a lot. He had a great sense of humor and was good friends with Fred Weigelt. We all got together for some social time one evening and had a lot of fun. I won't get into details, but I still remember going to bed that night and holding on to mattress as it spun around in circles.

Each Land Manager is responsible for the development, management and maintenance of wildlife habitat on state game lands and other public hunting grounds in several counties. As their title suggests, they are managers and have a

Food and Cover Corps to handle most of the physical work. Scottie and I didn't have to do any labor; we just drove around, touring the facilities at several game lands in Will's management area. It was a good assignment all in all, and we learned a lot about how to properly manage the forests, fields and wildlife on state owned properties.

As graduation approached, things started to ease up at the school. We had more free time, better weather, and started playing volleyball and baseball on slow afternoons. Superintendent Williams hardly ever used the term, *if and when you graduate* anymore and a future as a fulltime state game warden started to become a reality for us.

One of the primary topics of conversation among Trainees was where we'd like to be assigned upon graduation. We all had a wish list, with most desiring rural districts away from large metropolitan areas. The southeast region was one of the least desirable places to be assigned, especially knowing that Montgomery County was vacant, which included part of Philadelphia at the time. In early May, each student was called into the superintendent's office and asked where they would like to be transferred with no promises made to honor any requests. I was one of the few to ask for the Southeast Division, for I had promised my wife before I took the Civil Service test that if I made it into the class I'd request southeastern Pennsylvania so she could be close to her family.

I told Superintendent Williams that I was good with any district except Montgomery County and requested Lehigh County if possible.

We were not told about our assigned districts until the night before graduation, which had everyone frazzled for weeks. Then, much to my dismay, when we finally learned our new assignments, I found out I was assigned to Montgomery County. I was in absolute shock. How could that happen? There were seven open counties in the southeast region and I got the only one I didn't want!

John (left) and Bill (right) on The Rock with our wives on graduation day

On June 26, 1976, graduation day finally arrived. Arrangements were made by the staff for our wives and parents to come to the Training School for a tour and to attend the graduation ceremony, which was held at the DuBois Area Senior High School Auditorium. I remember sitting in my quarters, waiting for my family to arrive, feeling kind of low, when Assistant Superintendent, Dick Furry walked in (there were no doors, just an opening for one). I looked up and he nodded a hello.

"I just wanted you to know that Superintendent Williams did not choose Montgomery County for you," he said.

I didn't know what to say. It sure didn't make me feel any better, just all the more bewildered. What had I done to be punished like this? My brother got exactly what he asked for: a rural, mountainous county. Somehow, I ended up exactly where I didn't want to be: the big city!

I kept my disappointment hidden as best as possible, not wanting to ruin the day for my wife and parents who had traveled so far to wish me well. And I think the fact that I was finally done with the school and on my way to a career most can only dream of, helped me feel pretty good all in all.

After an extensive tour of the Training School and surrounding grounds with our guests, we all traveled to DuBois for the graduation ceremony and Presentation of Badges. Two-thousand had applied, and now twenty-five men proudly stood on stage at a high school auditorium in northwestern Pennsylvania and accepted their badges from the Assistant Superintendent of the Ross Leffler School of Conservation. Regardless of where we were assigned or how we might have felt about the districts chosen for us, we all became game wardens that day. And for my brother and me, a lifelong dream of a career working with wildlife had finally been fulfilled.

Life as an Urban Game Warden

My NEW DISTRICT IN MONTGOMERY COUNTY encompassed half of Philadelphia County, including everything north of Market Street. Land mass was approximately four hundred square miles, and with a population of over two million people, I had no idea what I was in for. Having grown up in neighboring Bucks County, I had watched the farms and woodlands slowly disappear over the years as more and more people moved in from the city. They called it the suburban sprawl, and within a decade most of the fields and forests where I hunted and trapped as a boy had turned into housing developments. Due to the tremendous population base, there were thousands of hunters living in my district. And with open land becoming more scarce each year, local hunters would oversaturate the few places left where they were allowed to hunt.

Along with the thousands of hunters came tens-of-thousands of non-hunters who had no background or education in wildlife whatsoever. Their lack of knowledge and, often, their fear of wild critters got them into conflicts with nature, and generated between two thousand and three thousand complaints annually for me. In those days, game wardens had their names and phone numbers listed in the digest of hunting and trapping regulations that was issued with every hunting license. Imagine that: one million hunters with access to a hundred-and-twenty game wardens statewide. Wardens in rural districts with low populations didn't get the same number of calls as their brother officers in urban districts, but still, it was challenging to have your home phone ringing off the hook all day long. Many officers had their wives fielding phone calls for them. In fact, it was expected by our supervisors. Maryann worked outside the home during the week, so she wasn't held hostage to dozens of calls each day, mostly about nuisance skunks, squirrels, groundhogs and what have you. And I couldn't stay home all day answering phone calls, especially during hunting season. But the calls didn't end when I got home at night. The folks who couldn't reach me during the day would call all night long, sometimes at two or three in the morning! My wife had weekends off, and tried her best to handle the phone calls for me when I was on patrol. If she couldn't, she would take their information and promise a call when I returned home. But the sheer number of phone calls soon became overwhelming for both of us.

This went on for years until the Game Commission purchased recorded answering devices for all game wardens. At first, I thought this would be a big improvement in my life. But I soon learned it made things worse in some ways, for when I got back from a long day on patrol, I'd have twenty-five or thirty calls to return, and I'd spend hours on the phone with people complaining about raccoons in their chimneys, squirrels in the attic, deer eating their bushes, geese pooping on their lawns, skunks spraying in the neighborhood, roadkilled deer, and whatnot. Every once in a while I'd get a call about a hunting violation, but most of them were safety zone infractions (hunting within one hundred fifty yards of an occupied building). Thing is, there were so many houses surrounding open fields it would be difficult to stay clear of a safety zone. And for many homeowners, the mere sight of a hunter, even if he was five hundred yards away, would be enough to call the game warden. I'd even get complaints at the mere sound of gunshots in the distance.

But there were also times when safety zone complaints were more than valid. One that I'll always remember was when my brother-in-law, Curt, called me because a bullet had entered his house.

Curt lived across the street from me, so I went right over to investigate. He told me that he saw three hunters walking abreast in a hayfield bordering his property when a buck was jumped. He watched one man raise his rifle and fire three shots as the fleeing deer ran broadside to his house. One of the bullets went through an outside wall and sailed directly into a bedroom where Curt's two-year-old son was sleeping. The bullet traveled between the rails of the child's crib as he slept. Had his son been standing, he could have been killed, for the bullet would have struck him in the head.

The deadly missile went through another wall into the back of a dresser in Curt's bedroom and lodged inside a heavy blanket. The projectile was in excellent shape, for it hadn't expanded all that much, even after penetrating the exterior of Curt's house, and I was able to determine that the hunter was using a .30 caliber firearm. Because a forensic ballistics test would be possible, all I needed was the gun and I'd have a rock solid case.

Since I'd been able to get to the scene in a matter of minutes, I figured I had a good chance of catching the person responsible. I knew there were three men, and unless they had returned home for the day, odds were in my favor. Curt was able to give me a little information about them: all three wore orange vests and hats, all three were white males, but the one who fired had a short, chin beard while the other two were clean shaven. They were approximately a hundred yards from his house when the shot was fired, too far to get a better description of them.

I called for backup and soon had several deputies arrive. Two immediately went into the surrounding fields and woods in search of the men while the third went out to the county road with me. I planned to check every vehicle I saw, and because it was a relatively rural area and the road seldom traveled, I had no reservations about making vehicle stops. As luck would have it, a car carrying three orange-clad men soon came down the road from the general direction of Curt's house, and I signaled for it to stop.

I stepped over to the driver's window and immediately suspected it was them. All were hunters, which was obvious from their dress, and one had a chin beard, just as Curt had described.

"Something wrong, officer?" asked the driver.

"Were you three hunting in this area a little while ago?" I asked.

"Yes," said the driver, "but we didn't get a deer, if that's what you're looking for."

"Did you see any?"

"We did see a buck. Fred shot at it but he missed."

The man with a chin beard nodded solemnly. "It was a nice one, too."

I looked at Fred. "Do you have identification with you?"

"Yes," he said. "But why are you asking all these questions? We didn't do anything wrong."

I began to suspect that the men had no idea Fred's bullet had entered someone's home. Don't ask me how to explain it, but they didn't look or act guilty. Just surprised that I had stopped them. I asked Fred what kind of rifle he was using.

"It's a Remington thirty-aught-six," he said.

I pointed to my right. "Were you hunting in the field over there?"

"Yes. That's where we saw the deer."

"Did you see the house, too? There's only one on that side of the road."

"Yes, but we were nowhere near it," insisted Fred. "Is that what this is about? Some anti-hunter complaining that we were on his property?"

"I know the man," I said. "He wasn't an anti-hunter before but he might be now. Your bullet went into his house. Could have killed his son."

A look of shock crossed the faces of all three men. "No way!" insisted Fred. "I never shot toward that house!"

"They were home when you shot at the deer," I said. "The owner watched you shoot at it from the kitchen window and discovered the bullet hole a short while later. Had to be you."

Fred shook his head violently. "Nope! Wasn't me. There's lots of hunters around today. Bullets can travel for miles. Could've been anybody."

I looked at the driver. "Guns in the trunk?"

He nodded a yes.

"Step out and open it for me."

The driver got out, walked around the vehicle and popped open the trunk. There were three rifles, one was a Remington .30-06 which belonged to Fred.

I turned to my deputy. "Take all three rifles and put them in my car. Bring back three receipts with the make, model and serial number of each gun written on it."

"You can't do that!" complained the driver. "We didn't do anything wrong. Why are you taking all of our rifles?"

"I'm going to send all three to the State Police Crime Lab. They'll run a ballistics check on each rifle to determine which one shot through the house."

"But—!"

I cut him off. "Look, all three rifles are thirty caliber. The bullet was a thirty caliber. You all admitted hunting here earlier and Fred admitted shooting at a deer. I'm going to have all three rifles checked to be certain we have the right one. You'll have your guns returned when I hear back from the state police."

"How long will that take?"

"Probably at least a month."

He opened his mouth to speak and I put up my hand. "There's nothing you can say that will change my mind. I'm sorry it has to be this way but I don't have a choice. Now please get back in your car. I want to see hunting licenses and identification from all three of you."

As it turned out, the crime lab was able match the bullet with Fred's rifle, and I filed citations against all three men for hunting in a safety zone with an additional charge against Fred for damaging property. Fred's total fine was fifty dollars, twenty-five for the safety zone and twenty-five for damaging property while hunting. In those days, that's all I could do, for there was no other game law violation that covered shooting into a house.

Inexcusable as they may be, line-of-fire incidents like this occur because the offender focuses entirely on his target and nothing else. Fred was so excited about the prospect of bagging a deer that he might never have seen the house directly behind it. I'll never forget the time my brother and I were setting traps for muskrats when we were in our early teens. It during pheasant season in the mid-1960s (these were the days when muskrats and ring-necked pheasants were everywhere in Pennsylvania), and we had just walked from a streambed into a grassy field when we saw two hunters coming our way. I spotted a male ring-neck crouched in the high grass and raised my hand to alert the hunters. "There's a pheasant just ahead," I called out. "I'll jump him for you." With that, I started walking toward the hunters and flushed the bird, expecting them to wait until it was safe to shoot. Instead, one hunter raised his muzzle as the airborne pheasant was level with my head. John and I were directly in the line of fire and both dropped to the ground as the hunter blasted away. In his apparent excitement, he forgot all about us, his mind focusing entirely on the bird.

Scientific studies have shown that instances of intense, psychological emotion can lead to tunnel vision, which causes someone to sharply narrow his field of vision so that he is visualizing his surroundings as if looking through the scope on a hunting rifle. This may explain how Fred shot at a deer when the house behind it was plainly visible and in his direct line of fire.

It was my belief that Fred didn't see a true picture of his surroundings, just like the pheasant hunter when I was a boy. Instead, Fred saw only the fleeing buck due to an overwhelming desire for a kill, and when confronted with the fact that his bullet went through someone's house, he refused to believe it.

I am convinced that if every hunter practiced two basic rules of safe hunting, far fewer incidents like this would happen. The first rule is to positively identify your target before you pull the trigger. The second is to be sure there is nothing in your line of fire. As detailed above, under the right circumstances, your mind can deceive you. Although most hunters are careful and take plenty of time to absorb what they see, some don't. They simply react. As a result, each year occupied homes are shot into and humans are shot in mistake for game, often bringing tragic results to both the victim and the offender.

As stated earlier, safety zone complaints were common during hunting season, with dozens of calls coming across my desk or over the airwaves of my Game Commission radio each week. But of all the hundreds of calls, another that was etched in my memory concerned a police chief and his hunting buddy.

I had received a phone call from a gentleman explaining that he lived on a dead-end road bordering a large vacant field, and that pheasant hunters were getting too close over the past week, with one peppering his house with shotgun pellets. I promised I'd try to help and drove out there early on the following Saturday. After parking my patrol car at the end of a road bordering the field, I waited. It didn't take long before a lone pheasant hunter came into view. He was a good two hundred yards away, walking slowly toward the complainant's house with his shotgun held in a two-handed ready position, when he suddenly pointed his muzzle toward the ground and fired. At first, I had no idea what he was shooting at, but seconds later the pungent odor of skunk musk filled the air as he continued walking toward the house with his shotgun held at the ready.

I have to admit, there was something about his manner that bothered me. I disliked the fact that he'd killed something without giving it a second glance and simply moved on, hoping to flush a bird. I waited until he was about a hundred yards away when I walked to the edge of the field in full uniform and called him over. Ejecting three rounds from his shotgun, he placed them into his pocket and shuffled toward me.

"Is there a problem, officer?" he asked. He was in his mid-fifties. His tone was gruff, his face exhibiting impatience.

"You're hunting in a safety zone."

He swiveled his head left and right. "I don't see any signs."

"Doesn't have to be posted," I said. I nodded toward the complainant's house. "It's illegal to hunt within a hundred and fifty yards of occupied buildings."

"I didn't know that."

"It's in the digest you get with your hunting license along with other common violations," I said. "You should read it sometime."

From the corner of my eye, I noticed another hunter walking toward us in long, powerful strides. His break-action shotgun was open and carried in his right hand as he approached. I turned to face him.

"What's the problem here?" he said sharply. "I'm the chief of police for this township and this man is my friend."

He was arrogant, his tone indicating his superiority—that I should turn around and leave them alone. It got my hackles up. After all, we both wore badges and we both enforced the law. But I could see the contempt in his face and knew things would only get worse from here. This wasn't the first time I'd run into a situation like this. I was stuck in the middle of the biggest metropolitan area in the state. As a result, some police officers regarded me as an intruder in their territory. The fact that I was a state officer only served to rankle them all the more. If there were any laws broken, *they* were the ones who would handle it, not some dopy bunny cop!

"I want to see your hunting license," I said to the chief. It wasn't a request, but an order, and he knew it.

"You want to see my hunting license! Do you know who I am? I'm Chief Glutton. This is *my* township, pal!"

I was in my twenties. He was in his fifties. That had to anger him all the more. No way did he want some rookie telling him what to do.

"I don't care if you own the whole county," I said. "You can comply or I'll charge you with resisting inspection of a state officer."

I watched his cheeks turn beet red. He was ready to explode. "You are gonna pay for this!" he warned as he turned to show me the license on his back. I pulled it from the holder, looked it over and stuck it back inside. I could have demanded to see some identification but I thought I'd pushed it far enough. There was no doubt in my mind that he was the Chief, and I already knew there would be repercussions, but at the time, I just didn't care.

I tuned to the other man. "I want to see your hunting license and your identification."

After witnessing my exchange with Chief Glutton, he had no intention of stoking my flaming mood. He pulled out a wallet and handed me his driver's license. Then he turned so I could examine the hunting license on his back. After jotting down the information I needed for a citation, I handed both items back to him.

"I'm going to file charges against you for hunting in a safety zone," I told him. "You'll receive a citation in the mail in a few days."

Chief Glutton couldn't contain himself any longer. "You'll see us in court!" he roared. "And I'll be sure to tell the judge about your disrespectful attitude!"

I was still new in my district and had no idea how close the ties could be with local law enforcement and certain judges. So when it was time for our day in court, I brought the complainant in as a witness, and he testified about the constant barrage of hunters shooting too close to his house, explaining that he'd had shotgun pellets raining down on his roof on several occasions.

The judge sat at his bench stone-faced and silent. And when my witness finished testifying, I took the stand and went into detail about the hunter being too close to a house when he shot at a skunk and that as he continued toward the house with his shotgun at the ready, I called him over and explained that he was in violation of the Game Law.

When I finished testifying, the defendant took the stand. He brought Chief Glutton with him, but the chief never said a word. What I didn't know, was that the chief had met with the judge earlier and the fix was in. The defendant didn't have much to say, other than admitting he was hunting pheasants that day but claimed that he was more than a hundred and fifty yards from the house when I called him over to me. So it was his word against mine. And in cases like these, the judge almost always rules in favor of the lawman. But as a young officer, I'd made a slight error, in that I should have walked out to the hunter and marked off the area so I would have had a measuring point back to the house. Instead, I'd called him over to me because I didn't want to pick up any skunk spray on my boots. But when I walked back into the field later that day with a tape measure, expecting to mark the distance from the dead skunk back to the house, I couldn't find the carcass. Apparently, the defendant's aim was off, and he'd either missed the animal entirely or only wounded it, enabling the skunk to crawl off. Fortunately, I was able to find his ejected shell casing from when he fired at the skunk and measured from there. However, that wasn't good enough for the judge, and he found Chief Glutton's buddy not guilty. But when he followed up with an attack on my character, accusing me of being a bully and disrespecting the police, I knew Chief Glutton was behind it.

There were other instances of contempt for the Game Commission demonstrated by township police departments, but for the most part, I had a good relationship with the law enforcement officers in my district, especially the state police and the Philadelphia Police Department. But one of the most egregious displays of contempt for my authority came from a police chief and a judge in a semi-rural area of my otherwise urban district.

I had cited a young male in his early twenties named Tom Cannon for a littering violation, and he refused to respond to the citation by asking for a hearing or simply paying the twenty-five dollar fine. Eventually, a clerk at the judge's office issued a warrant for his arrest and mailed it to me. Serving arrest warrants can be a dangerous business. And to make matters worse, we hadn't received any instructions on proper procedures from the Training School. Nor were we encouraged to run criminal background checks through the National Crime Information Center for those named on arrest warrants. As a result, I'd have a warrant for someone charged with a game law violation, with no idea if the individual had a violent criminal background.

In this particular case, I was on patrol during small game season and took a drive by Cannon's house (he lived with his mother) when I spotted his car parked in the driveway. I'd been after him for weeks, so I immediately pulled to the roadside and parked my patrol car. I was in full uniform when I went to the front door and knocked. But when his mother came to the door, she told me her son wasn't home. She was dressed in a terrycloth bathrobe and clutching it together at the neck.

"That's Tom's car parked in the driveway, isn't it?" I said.

"Yes, but he's not here."

"I have a warrant for his arrest," I said. "Tell him to come out or I'll have to come inside for him."

"I said he's not here!" she said sharply and began to close the door. I quickly stuck my foot inside and it bounced back at her. "You can't come in here!" she cried, eyes wild with panic. "I told you my son isn't home!" She tried to close the door again but my foot was still inside.

I could have forced my way in, but considering she was only wearing a bathrobe, holding it together in one hand while pushing the door against my boot with the other, I figured it would be better if I left. "Have your son contact me," I said. Then I slid my foot from the doorway and walked back to my patrol car.

But as I was about to drive off, Canon came strolling out the front door and walked over to me. "What are you harassing my mother for?" he said angrily.

"I have a warrant for your arrest," I said. "You can pay your fine now or I'll be taking you with me."

"I ain't going nowhere with you. The cops are on their way right now."

I was taken aback. "You called the police?"

"Mom did."

I heard the wail of emergency sirens in the distance. They were getting closer by the second. I couldn't believe it. Here I was in full uniform with a marked patrol car and a warrant for her son's arrest...and she calls the police. It was part and parcel of being an urban game warden, as most folks didn't look at us as "real" law enforcement officers.

The police came quick: two township patrol cars racing toward me with their red lights ablaze, sirens blaring against the quiet morning breeze. Both cars slowed when they saw my marked sedan. They parked. One in front of it, the other behind, blocking me in a show of force.

They exited their police cars and walked over to us. "Game warden!" one remarked in confusion. "We got a call about a man trying to break into the house!"

I pulled the warrant from my back pocket and handed it to him. He looked it over and turned his attention to Cannon. "Your mother should have told us about this." He placed his hand on Tom Cannon's shoulder. Get in the car, son. You're going to see the judge, right now."

Cannon sat in the back of the car, but he wasn't in cuffs, which gave me the sneaking suspicion that the police had some kind of personal connection with him.

I followed the cars for about a mile when they turned into the local district justice's office and parked. Tom Cannon got out with them and we all walked into the judge's chambers. It was a Saturday. Judges don't work on Saturdays unless they're on call, and this judge was not on call that weekend. I expected him to be in a foul mood toward the defendant as a result. It was a beautiful autumn day, and the judge could have been home relaxing or out on the golf course, instead he was sitting in his chambers with a scowl on his flabby cheeks, glaring at me.

"Don't you have anything better to do than harass this man and scare the dickens out of his mother?" he scolded.

I was shocked. Angry too. The person he should have leveled his displeasure toward was the accused lawbreaker, not me! "I have a warrant for his arrest, Your Honor," I said. "I drove by his house and saw his car parked outside—"

"I DON'T CARE WHAT YOU SAW!" he boomed. He took a deep breath, nostrils flaring like a racehorse in the

Kentucky Derby. "You should have contacted the police chief and asked him to have one of his officers take care of this. Next time, make sure you do!"

I kept quiet, knowing it would only bring more hostility my way if I said anything.

He looked at the defendant. "Tommy," he said evenly, "these officers are going to take you back home. But first you have to assure me you'll take care of this matter. This man has a warrant for your arrest for failing to appear in court. You have to arrange for a hearing…or you can just plead guilty, I don't care, but you can't continue to ignore this thing. Do you understand me?"

"Yes, sir."

"Good. Now get out of here."

The whole thing was ridiculous. But what could I do? Any attempt to argue with the judge would only serve to hurt me the next time I brought a case before him. So I let it go, got back in my patrol car and resumed my patrol. Small game season was in full swing and hunting pressure was heavy. There was plenty to do rather than fume over the way I'd just been treated.

A few hours later, a Game Commission dispatcher called to inform me that Tom Cannon wanted to meet me right away to pay his fine. I was surprised to hear it, but also glad the matter was coming to a close. I told the dispatcher to have Cannon meet me in the parking lot of a diner that was close to his house. Noon was approaching, and I thought I'd get lunch after settling up with him.

On my way to the diner, I stopped and picked up my dear friend, Deputy Bob McConnell. He sat in the back of my patrol car as I pulled into the diner and parked. Tom Cannon was standing outside and came right over, so I motioned for him to sit up front with me.

Cannon opened the passenger door and slid inside. "I got the money," he said. "Twenty-five dollars cash."

"That's fine," I told him. "But you understand you can have a hearing in front of a judge if you want."

He nodded that he understood.

I handed him a field acknowledgement of guilt for littering, then said, "Read it and sign it and we're done."

Cannon never bothered to read anything. He simply signed his name on the dotted line and pulled twenty-five dollars out of a pocket in his jeans. But instead of handing it to me, he set the money on the dashboard, which struck me as odd. I reached up and took the cash, then handed him a copy of the field acknowledgment he'd signed. "We're done," I said. "You can go."

Tom Cannon opened the door then looked back at me with a silly grin on his face.

"Something wrong?" I asked.

"Nope. Everything is good," he said. Then he slid out the door and slammed it shut.

Deputy McConnell and I got out of my car and started walking toward the diner when two men exited an unmarked vehicle that had been parked in front of my car in a spot where it wouldn't be readily noticed. One wore a sports coat and tie. The other, a much younger man, wore jeans and a plaid shirt. The older man produced a badge and showed it to us. "Chief Twit," he said. "Township police. I want to talk to you about the incident we just observed."

It came to me in a flash: the whole thing was a setup. The chief was hoping to catch us in a shakedown, which is why Cannon had put his fine money on the dashboard. The chief and his subordinate wanted to make sure they saw me physically take the cash.

I showed him a copy of the paper Cannon had signed. "He plead guilty and signed this," I said. "It's a Game Commission field acknowledgement. We settle a lot of cases this way."

"In a parking lot!" scoffed the chief. "You take money off of people in a parking lot and call that legal!"

It was the last straw. I had no time for any more insults or silly games from the local judge or the local police. I looked at the chief and shook my head in resentment. "If you want to arrest me, go ahead. Otherwise I'm going inside to have lunch with my deputy." We stood there staring at each other for a moment, then I turned my back to him and walked inside the diner with McConnell.

I never heard another word from the police chief or the judge after that day, and tried to stay out of their township whenever I could. Still, there were times when I would apprehend a violator there, and I'd always settle with them on a field acknowledgment of guilt rather than risk bringing a case in front of a judge whom I considered to be hostile toward Game Commission officers.

Because I was assigned to Montgomery and Philadelphia Counties, I started getting arrest warrants forwarded to me from game wardens all over the state. I was expected to serve these warrants for them and physically arrest anyone who didn't have the money to pay their fine. Once arrested, the defendants had to be transported back to the county in which the violation occurred, which in some cases was over a hundred miles away. Some of the arrest warrants were for trivial matters like camping on state game lands—a ten dollar fine. And I was expected to find the campers and physically arrest them, even if it meant going into the bowels of center city Philadelphia to track them down. Those warrants were put on the bottom of the heap.

I served more than a hundred arrest warrants over the years, with many in the city of Philadelphia. Fortunately, the Philadelphia Police Department was always there to help. It was a novelty for them to meet up with a state game warden and go after someone for shooting a deer rather than a human, and most of the officers actually enjoyed assisting me. They would always send a paddy wagon (a type of van used by police officers for transporting prisoners) and a separate patrol car to meet me on the outskirts of the city. I'd show the officers my warrant and they would lead me to the house and assist me in every way possible as backup. It was so good to have them come along. I almost always served arrest warrants at night, when I was more likely to find folks at home. The city is so big and congested and dark that I doubt I would have found most of the defendants if it hadn't been for my police escorts. And they would always be at my side when I knocked at a door, entering the house with me and assisting in the physical arrest. If the defendant couldn't pay the fine, he would be brought outside in handcuffs, loaded into the paddy wagon, and taken downtown where he'd be placed in a holding cell with other incarcerated men until the judge was ready to see them. In those days, it was mandatory that anyone picked up on a warrant in Philadelphia be taken before a Municipal Court Judge before they could be transported out of the city.

The holding cell for suspects who were arrested and brought in by the police was at the lower level of the municipal building, and their cases were reviewed regularly. The suspects, along with my prisoner, would be lined up—as many as fifteen or twenty at a time—and handcuffed to a long chain, before being taken from the cell and marched upstairs to see the judge.

In my case, there was no hearing or opportunity for my defendant to address the judge. My job was to show the municipal judge the arrest warrant before I could take him to a jail in the county where the violation occurred. Some of the municipal court judges had no idea what a game warden was. I remember well the time I followed a chain gang of men upstairs and had a judge ask to see my identification before he'd let me take my prisoner out of the city. I was in full uniform. There was a badge on my chest. I showed him a lawful arrest warrant signed by a judge in a different county, and yet he still wanted me to show him some kind of identification. Fortunately, I had an ID card in my wallet issued by the Game Commission, which satisfied his bewilderment.

Nuisance Wildlife Complaints an Everyday Affair

ALTHOUGH LAW ENFORCEMENT WAS a priority for me, most of my time in the so called "off season" was spent answering wildlife complaints. And there was nothing I disliked more than the annual goose roundup in summer.

Montgomery County is sprinkled liberally with expansive country estates, well-manicured country clubs and huge business campuses. Some of the wealthiest people in the nation live here. Hence, many of the country clubs are the finest to be found anywhere, and the business campuses are some of the largest and richest in the world. These properties are landscaped to flawless perfection by master gardeners and carpeted with lush, emerald grasses painstakingly cared for by professional greenskeepers. And along with the gorgeous floral bouquets and sunken gardens found on these professionally designed properties that combine nature and culture, there is always a pond or two, which makes a perfect place for Canada geese to thrive.

Migrating geese would stop by to feed on the grasses in these places as they made their way south each spring. But some chose to stay year round. And it was here that they would build their nests and raise their young. The goslings, having been born here, would stay as well. And the population would grow a little more each year until the turf damage and goose droppings on the properties would be more than folks could bear.

The complaints would begin to filter in as early as March. By summer, there would be a dozen or more, and it would take a wagon train of Game Commission trucks to transport all the men required to round up the nuisance birds. It took two full days to catch all the geese. One of reasons was the traffic. I was always the lead car, and the caravan of trucks would follow me throughout the county from one location to another, with the average day bringing us through a hundred traffic lights or more.

Another frequent problem was neighbor disputes. Sometimes a large flock of geese would occupy two properties separated by a single body of water. One neighbor would want the geese and the other would not. I once watched two women go nose-to-nose after we arrived as they argued whether or not the geese should be taken. For a moment, I thought it would come to blows, so we got back in our vehicles and left the premises rather than add to their brewing hostility.

Each year, in late June or early July, Canada geese molt, leaving them flightless for ten days to two weeks while their new wing feathers grow in. This was when we would go after them. Heading the birds into a makeshift corral, we'd pick them up, one by one, and put them in wooden crates to be shipped south. Game wardens from Georgia, South Carolina, North Carolina and Alabama would make the long trip to Pennsylvania each summer to help collect our nuisance geese so they could release them along their southern waterways where the Canada goose population had all but disappeared.

It was always hot during the goose roundup, and we had to be concerned about the birds overheating, so we would look for a shady area to stake down our temporary corral consisting of a reinforced chicken wire fence fashioned into a V taper. Once it was erected, a gang of us would go after the geese.

Most times we'd catch them on land and it would be easy to herd the birds into the corral. But sometimes the geese would run into a large body of water and we'd have to launch canoes. Geese can outmaneuver canoes, so it took considerable skill to chase them back on land. Poison ivy was another constant problem. Canada geese seem to thrive in it. I think they eat the stuff. Luckily, I'm not allergic, wish I could say the same for the others. Some of the men got it really bad. Discourteous golfers were a constant threat too, their little white balls whizzing overhead as we marched into the greens to surround the geese—as many a hundred at a time—and slowly drive them into our corral. Once inside, we would close it off, leaving two men inside the pen. They would grab a goose in each hand, holding them by the shoulders as they lifted the birds over to the men outside the corral. I found out the hard way that geese can really bite if you're careless. They have long necks, too, and can reach places on your body you don't want reached.

Those of us on the outside would put the birds in wooden crates that held eight to ten birds each. Others carried the crates to a large flatbed truck to be stacked atop each other. This got tricky as the crates began to pile up. Lifting them over your head while simultaneously dodging a fusillade of boiling goose poop is an art few can master, including me. I soon learned firsthand what the adage *loose as a goose* was all about.

Finally, after loading up the geese, we would drive off amidst cheers of onlookers. But it was always disheartening for me to see such a noble bird caged and reduced to common sweepings.

I'll forever remember the time we were heading to a location to catch geese when I got a radio call about a deer that jumped a chain-link fence surrounding a storage yard for a propane gas company. I was leading my caravan of goosebusters when the call came over my Game Commission radio. Since we were close by, I decided to proceed directly to the scene.

When we arrived, the terrified deer was running back and forth along the fence in a futile attempt to escape. The fence was only five feet high, and could easily have been hurdled, but the crazed whitetail, blind with panic, never even tried.

I had left my tranquilizer gun at home, and my initial hope, upon first entering the yard, was that there would be a gate I could open to free the deer. Unfortunately, the only gate was at the opposite side of the yard, far from the trapped whitetail, and led directly to a highway.

The deer appeared to be a yearling, weighing perhaps 50 pounds, so I thought I'd try wrestling it to the ground and then hog-tie it. I was lifting weights at the gym every day and weighed a solid 220 pounds. Having a crowd of men with me who could help once I had it down made the idea seem all the more plausible.

The deer was running along the fence at full speed until it smashed into the opposite side, at which point it would immediately turn, charge in the other direction, and smash into that side.

It did this repeatedly as I cautiously approached and concealed myself behind a row of shrubbery. Twice the deer passed within inches of me before I was set; then, as it came by for the third time, I lunged from my cover and grabbed for it. But the deer knocked me on my backside as if I were made of cardboard. Tackling a three-hundred-pound linebacker would have been an easier task.

On the positive side, my fumbled maneuver caused the deer to turn and run toward the center of the yard where it was blocked by long rows of propane gas cylinders. The frantic whitetail tried to leap over them but only made it halfway across before falling into the steel bottles, causing them to topple like dominoes in every direction. Unable to gain solid footing on their rounded surfaces, the deer floundered helplessly.

Seeing an opportunity to make our move, several of us waded into the cylinders, wrestled the bewildered animal to the ground, and managed to hogtie it. With the deer securely hobbled, we carried it over to a Game Commission vehicle and transported it into a wooded area a short distance away.

A long with all the complaints about geese, skunks, squirrels, raccoons and other "nuisance" animals, I had more than my share of deer incidents. But one stands out indelibly in my mind. It was a Sunday afternoon during the month of March, when I received a call about a deer trapped inside a car dealership. I usually take Sundays off, but every game warden soon realizes how precariously insecure scheduled days off can be in our line of work.

I jumped in my uniform, raced out the front door, and climbed into my Chevy Blazer. Having since learned my lesson, I now carried a tranquilizer gun in my vehicle at all times. Of course, the mere fact that you have one at your disposal doesn't necessarily guarantee success. Unlike the countless number of television programs depicting everything from small mammals to rampaging rhinos being subdued instantly by one of these dart-flinging rifles, tranquilizer guns aren't all they're cracked up to be.

Whenever I respond to an incident about a deer being someplace it shouldn't, I whisper a little prayer that it's gone before I arrive. I couldn't remember a single time when that worked for me, but I said one anyway as I rolled into the small town of Hatboro.

As I stepped out of my patrol car, Bill Wallace greeted me. Bill had a permit from the Game Commission to remove nuisance wildlife for the public. Because he was a highly recognized wildlife trapper working in both Bucks and Montgomery Counties, the police had summoned him to the scene as well.

Bill had been waiting for me. "I thought I'd hang around in case you wanted some help," he said.

I thanked him for his offer and grabbed my tranquilizer rifle and related equipment from my vehicle. As we walked toward the car dealership, a large crowd had gathered along with several police officers who were standing by. I noticed one of the garage door windows leading into the service area was missing and asked a patrolman about it.

"Can you believe it?" he said in amazement. "I don't know how an animal that big could've fit through that window, but that's how the deer got in!"

I had to agree. The window didn't look big enough for a deer to squeeze its body through, let alone make it on a flying leap. "If the deer got in through this window," I said, 'it might come out the same way. Better keep the crowd back while we're inside."

He nodded affirmatively "No problem, warden. We'll keep the area clear."

Bill and I entered through the front door of the shop and immediately spotted the deer. It was in the back of the building, eyeing us nervously. The garage contained a number of automobiles, many of them brand new, and the grim realization that a spooked deer could easily damage several of them made me a little nervous. A few banged up vehicles could tally a sizeable amount of money; on the other hand, if the deer managed to leap back outside through a garage window, innocent bystanders could be injured or a passing motorist might hit it, creating even more havoc. York Road passed within mere yards of the building and was heavily traveled.

In an attempt to avoid the latter, I asked Bill Wallace to stand by the garage door. "If the deer comes your way," I told him, "wave your arms and start hollering so it won't jump out through another window and hurt somebody."

"You got it," he said, and positioned himself several feet ahead of the garage door while I loaded my tranquilizer gun.

I set a tackle box full of darts and equipment on a nearby desk and popped it open. Each dart had to be carefully prepared before loading it into the rifle. It was a tedious procedure requiring the proper blend of several drugs. I was using a mixture that acted as a muscle relaxer, and carefully withdrew a measured amount with a syringe, then injected it into my dart by inserting the substance through its hollow barbed needle. Next, I affixed a thin rubber cap on the needle to retain the substance and carefully injected air into the dart's shaft with an empty syringe to add weight and help balance it in flight. Finally, I screwed on a plastic-feathered tailpiece and placed the missile into the chamber of my rifle.

The tranquilizer gun had a dial mounted to the chamber with a series of numbers on it. Each number represented the approximate distance the dart was supposed to travel. I adjusted the dial for close range and walked slowly toward the deer.

I only took a few steps when the whitetail bolted toward several parked cars. Fearing it might damage them, I dashed toward the deer, causing it to turn and run toward the garage door. I quickly shouldered my rifle and fired, but the dart only sailed over the deer's rump as it charged past me.

Bill waved his arms in the air and shouted an impressive Neanderthal roar as the frantic deer raced toward him. But instead of turning away, the whitetail attempted to jump over him. Losing its footing on the smooth concrete floor, the deer fell forward, its front legs landing across Bill's shoulders while it stood on its hind legs directly in front of him, creating the bizarre image of a twosome about to dance the mambo.

Suddenly the deer began pummeling Bill's shins with its hooves in a desperate attempt to climb over him. Bill tried to stay upright but the whitetail knocked him to the concrete floor, its full weight on top of him.

The bewildered deer quickly leaped off Bill and charged toward the garage door. Again and again, the crazed deer smashed into the bottom windows only to bounce back each time. They had been replaced years ago with hardened Plexiglas and were impossible to penetrate.

Bill stumbled to his feet and both of us sprinted back to the opposite end of the garage. Three garage windows were now covered with blood, and I saw more blood on the deer's face as circled back and ran by us.

I asked Bill if he was okay. He was, and we decided to try the same thing over again. Actually, there wasn't anything else we could do, short of killing the deer, and neither of us wanted that.

I went back to my tackle box, prepared another dart, and loaded it into the rifle. This time I adjusted it to shoot lower by turning back the numbered dial.

Once more, I slowly approached the trapped whitetail, hoping it would stand still long enough to get a decent shot. But just as I was about to take aim, the deer bolted toward the garage door again. I fired from my hip as the deer passed within a few feet of me. It was a direct hit, but the dart only bounced off its muscular rump, spewing its liquid sedative into the air in a prolonged arc

I watched helplessly as the beleaguered whitetail charged toward my companion for the second time. Bill stood his ground, waving his arms in a desperate attempt to ward off another assault, but the frantic deer stormed onward and I worried Bill would be trampled or knocked flat by the animal, perhaps realizing a broken bone or some other serious injury.

Just as the deer was upon him, it jumped six feet into the air. It cleared Bill easily and landed squarely upon the concrete floor behind him. The terrified deer made another terrific leap, crashed through a glass window near the top of the garage door, and landed on the sidewalk outside the building. Again the animal vaulted forward, hurdling two cars parked bumper to bumper along the street before charging blindly into the front fender of a passing motorist.

The deer slumped to the ground like a flattened prizefighter, and for a moment seemed finished, but it suddenly sprang to its feet and bolted across the road, disappearing behind a building in the distance. Bill and I searched unsuccessfully for the animal, finally concluding that the deer must have ran back to its home range.

We were both relieved the episode was over, but I couldn't help thinking about all the things I might have done differently to improve the day's outcome. It didn't take long to realize that under the circumstances, Bill Wallace and I had made out rather well, for I was forgetting about a very common rule: whenever you deal with wildlife, anything can happen. And it usually does.

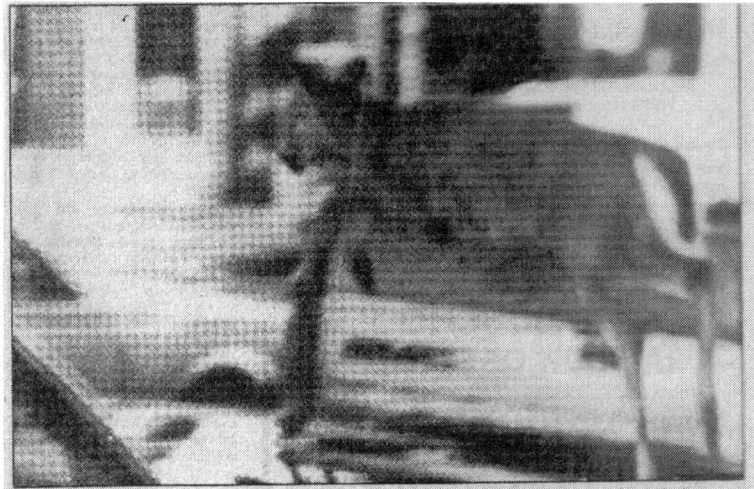

Photographer Patricia Gershanick was able to snap this shot of a leaping fawn Sunday afternoon just after it crashed through a bay door window at Ernie Brown & Sons in Hatboro.

Drama on York Road

A terrified deer eludes rescue efforts

By Rebecca Felten

As the afternoon waned Sunday and the gray and cold of the day settled in, passersby gathered outside the service area of the Ernie Brown & Son Nissan dealership in the north end of Hatboro's business district.

Kids on bikes and skateboards, several motorists and neighbors peered through the glass of the service bay door, each trying to catch a glimpse of a young fawn that moments earlier had leaped across York Road and crashed through one of the shallow panels.

Blood from the cuts on the deer's face and head smeared the lower windows where she had tried in vain to get out.

Most concerned with the animal's safety were Bonnie Linden of Roslyn and Tom Pisut of Willow Grove, who had been driving south on York Road when the deer ran from the car lot across the street and made two leaps across York Road, narrowly missing their car. Linden said they could see that the deer's face was covered with blood as they watched it ram against a plexiglass panel trying to escape.

Linden ran to the nearby 7-Eleven to call police and Pisut ran to the police station to get help. Two separate calls were logged, bringing Sgt. John Kimball and Officer F. Robert Palmyra to the scene. The officers waited with the rest until Brown service manager Jim Scarpello arrived around 4:45 p.m. to let them inside.

The officers had alerted William Wasserman of the state Game Commission, who is authorized to tranquilize animals. As an interim measure, Wasserman dispatched Bill Wallace of Buxmont Wildlife Control, Warminster, who is licensed by the state to trap or kill troublesome wildlife.

Wallace and the officers went inside, walking slowly and carefully to avoid frightening the animal who they feared might try to charge the garage door. Wallace discovered the animal lying in a corner in the rear of the building, but it ran to the back of the auto bay where the crowd outside could see its little figure silhouetted against the back garage door.

Almost simultaneously, someone inside leaned on a button which raised the rear door. Onlookers waited in anticipation to see if the deer would run, but it fled to another area.

*Please turn to page 2

Photographer gets a snapshot of the deer leaping over parked cars

Hunting Accidents

ALTHOUGH NUISANCE WILDLIFE COMPLAINTS consumed a lot of my time, there was also plenty of reason to be on patrol for game law violators. Because my district was heavily populated but had very little land open to hunting, I would see extremely heavy hunting pressure in places offering access to hunters. Evansburg State Park was just such a place. With a thousand acres open to hunting, it would become mobbed with hunters. Back then, the first day of pheasant and rabbit season started at nine o'clock in the morning, far later than other days of the season when legal hunting began a half hour before sunrise. Keep in mind, this was when our pheasant population (accompanied by heavy stocking) was near its peak in southeastern Pennsylvania, and there were tens of thousands of hunters from all over the state waiting for the opening day. In order to give everyone a fair chance at the birds, the Game Commission thought it best to have a nine o'clock opener.

I'll never forget driving my patrol car along the interior roadways in the Park just before opening hour. There would be hundreds of orange-clad hunters lined along the roads bordering the fields like soldiers about to go into battle, their parked vehicles jammed into every conceivable nook and cranny. It was an incredible sight, and along with the extreme hunting pressure in my district came a number of hunting accidents each year.

While it's an unpleasant task, piecing a hunting accident together can be intriguing. What caused it? How could it have been prevented? Did it occur by mere chance or develop out of sheer negligence?

I've learned over the years that hunting accidents are nearly always caused by negligence—negligence often fueled by greed. Unfortunately, some hunters measure the success of a hunt solely by the kill. Otherwise, they reason, the day is a loss. This is not what hunting should be all about.

Hunters that feel they *must* shoot something, and that if they come home empty-handed they've somehow become a lesser person, can be dangerous to hunt with. The wise sportsman chooses his hunting companions carefully, avoiding those who are out to prove they're the best "hunter" in the county. People like this are often too quick to pull the trigger.

Attitude means a lot when you have a gun in your hand. A firearm doesn't give you a second chance. It can't warn you if it's unwittingly pointed at a human being. There is no eraser on its end; your mistake won't go away.

Think about it. One tiny movement of your index finger can change your life forever. That's all it takes to kill someone.

It's not always the inexperienced hunter that causes hunting accidents, as many people think. Usually it's a male between the ages of twenty-one and fifty who has hunted most of his life. He is generally hunting with a shotgun, in broad daylight, for turkeys or small game when it happens.

Sound like anybody you know?

In essence, it all boils down to two types of people who are usually involved in hunting accidents: those who think they will never be shot and those who think they will never shoot anyone.

It's not that people who think they'll never be shot by another hunter believe in immortality; it's that they don't think. Period. They traipse through the woods happily believing hunting accident victims are always some nameless, faceless person they'll read about in the newspaper someday.

They believe this right up until the moment they're shot.

People who think they'll never shoot a human while hunting are usually the ones who do just that. They venture into the woods thinking they're incapable of it. But if you convince yourself that under the right circumstances, you could make such a mistake, the odds that it will never happen increase dramatically.

There are several hunting accidents that come to mind out of the dozens I investigated during my term in Montgomery County. One of the most regrettable was when an elderly grandfather shot at a pheasant and took out one of his grandson's eyes. This was similar to the hunter who almost shot my brother and me years earlier. A bird went up and grandad fired his shotgun as the bird was rising instead of waiting until he had a safe shot. Although he had taken his grandson hunting with him that day, his eagerness for success caused him to focus entirely on the bird (tunnel vision), affectively eliminating his grandson from his view. In other words, his brain, or mind's eye if you will, projected the image he *wanted* to see…no different than if he were watching a movie. Just him, the bird, and a great big world. But no grandson.

I investigated a number of similar cases involving overeager hunters. Another that comes to mind is an incident during deer season. I was covering western Montgomery County at the time, essentially managing three districts with over thirty deputies under me. Unlike eastern Montgomery County, which is in the Special Regulations Area where only buckshot can be used for deer, rifles were legal here.

Three hunters were involved. For the purpose of this story, I'll call them Ben, Tom and Joe. The three men were good friends. Ben and Tom worked together and had known each other for years. Tom was Joe's father.

Ben was driving deer for father and son who agreed to stay posted at the edge of wooded area until he came into view. Ben didn't mind being first to push his way up the brushy hill, even though he had gained a little too much weight this year and knew it would be difficult. He hoped to kick out some deer for his friends. He'd been a hunter for many years and thought he'd give them first crack at getting a nice buck.

It was a beautiful fall day: blue skies, a golden sun, and a cool breeze that kept him comfortable as he shuffled slowly uphill. Hunting pressure was heavy; he heard shots frequently.

But the thought that he might be hit by a bullet was the farthest thing from his mind. After all, he'd been hunting since he was a kid and never had a close call. Hunting accidents were something that happened to other guys, not to him. Besides, he had plenty of orange on. You could see him a mile away.

Ben finally got to the hilltop and stood for a moment to catch his breath. He could see Joe in a treestand about fifty yards away and waved to him. Joe waved back. Ben hadn't managed to push out a deer. He hadn't seen any and neither Tom or Joe had fired a shot. Maybe they'd hunt somewhere else, he thought. Distant shots could still be heard, indicating others were having success. Perhaps that was why they couldn't find a deer; they were in the wrong place.

Ben continued toward Joe until he reached his treestand. He leaned his firearm against the tree and reached up for Joe's rifle as he climbed down to greet him.

"Where's your dad," asked Ben.

"He moved to another spot. Got bored waiting for you," Joe added with a sly grin.

"Very funny."

"He's not too far," continued Joe. "Maybe fifty yards at the most. He saw some fresh rubs back there."

"Let's go find him and get out of here," suggested Ben as he picked up his rifle.

The two men started in Tom's direction and hadn't gotten far when they spooked a nice buck that had been bedded alongside a downed tree. Neither of them took a shot because it was running toward Joe's father. "Wow!" exclaimed Ben. "I hope your dad gets a—"

Ben's words were suddenly cut short when a shot rang out. It was close, followed by a second shot. Then another rattled through the woods, but Ben had been struck before he ever heard it.

At first, he didn't realize he'd been shot. It felt like a mule had kicked him. But there was no mule, just Joe and him. He was lying on his back, looking up through the canopy of trees at a brilliant, indigo sky. But what was he doing on his back? And why did it feel like his chest was caving in? Then he saw

Joe standing over him. He looked scared, and he was screaming for help…something about somebody being shot. That's when everything went black.

Soon Tom came storming out of the brushy undergrowth and knelt next to Ben. He could see a gaping hole in his friend's neck. A pool of blood on the ground next to him.

"What have I done!" he cried. "We have to get him to a hospital!"

Tom's bullets never did hit the deer, but his third shot struck Ben. The brush was so heavy he couldn't see him or his son even though they both had been wearing orange coats and hats. His .308 caliber bullet put an ugly gash across Ben's cheek and entered his neck, barely missing his carotid artery before passing within a quarter inch of his spinal column as it exited through his back. If Tom had moved his muzzle a hair to the left when he pulled the trigger, he would have shot Ben through the head. What's more, his deadly slug had missed Joe by mere inches. And the sickening thought that he could have killed his son made Tom's stomach churn.

I visited Ben in the hospital after his surgery. Fortunately, he made a full recovery and remained friends with Tom and Joe since the accident. No charges were filed in this case, since it was impossible for Tom to see the other two hunters in the densely wooded area where they stood. Although no laws were broken, I've always thought that hunting by driving deer was inherently unsafe. With this method, a hunter or group of hunters walks through the woods creating a ruckus, causing the deer to run away from them. Other hunters are posted along a perimeter where they'll be able to shoot the fleeing deer as they approach. Not only is this a common method of hunting big game, it is, in my opinion, one of the most potentially dangerous as well.

Often the hunters on stand see the spooked deer coming long before the drivers are visible. When hunting hilly, brushy, or wooded terrain, drivers dressed in florescent orange can be out of sight of their companions while in the direct line of fire. When driving for deer, it is extremely important that every member of the hunting party knows where their companions will be at all times. The opportunity to shoot a deer can be exciting, but don't let the excitement get the best of you. Be sure of your target, your zone of fire and what lies beyond before pulling the trigger. Had Tom followed that basic tenet, Ben would never have been shot that day.

It was only two days later that I investigated another hunting accident where someone was shot in mistake for a deer. Three hunters were involved, and I'll call them Fred, Dick, and Harry for the purpose of this story.

Fred was hunting by himself that fateful day when he saw Dick and Harry coming his way. They were behind him, a good hundred yards away, so he didn't think much of it, other than hoping they didn't see that nice eight-pointer before he did. He'd scouted the area earlier in the fall and had seen several nice bucks, but the one he wanted was a dandy and its head would make a fine trophy for his den.

Before long, Dick and Harry were directly behind Fred, and although a mere forty yards separated them, the hunters could not see him in his camouflage clothing. And because they were on private, posted property, owned by Harry's uncle, neither of them suspected anyone was there but themselves. How could they know that Fred had snuck into the woods before daybreak? They thought they had the whole place to themselves. So when something moved ahead of them, Dick and Harry stood frozen, watching breathlessly, hoping it was the big buck they were after.

"I saw something!" said Dick.
"Yeah. Me too," agreed Harry.
"Think it's him?"
"Shush! Let's wait a second."

Fred glanced back over his right shoulder when he heard Dick and Harry talking. They were going to ruin any chance of seeing the buck, and he was becoming annoyed. He shifted his weight and looked back at them, and was getting ready to shout out when he saw the rifle pointed his way.

Dick's 30.06 rifle was aimed at the brush as he waited for the buck to show itself, and when Fred squirmed around to signal them, Dick squeezed off a round at the movement.

It felt like a cannon ball when the bullet slammed into Fred's left shoulder and knocked him to the ground. He screamed out in pain, and both Dick and Harry ran to his aid.

The bullet went clean through Fred's shoulder and exited his collarbone, shattering it. Dick put pressure on the exit wound to stop the bleeding while Harry ran back to the car and drove to the closest phone booth (no cell phones back then) to call for an ambulance. Both men stood by until it arrived.

Fred lived. He was lucky. I visited him in the hospital later that day and got a full statement from him along with additional statements from Dick and Harry. Afterwards, I had Dick accompany me to the scene of the shooting and explain what happened. When I saw where he'd been standing and where Fred was sitting when he was shot, it surprised me. The distance was so close. Suspecting Fred's lack of orange clothing had contributed to the incident, I returned the following day with a deputy dressed in camouflage clothing. The deputy sat where Fred had been when he was shot while I stood where Dick was when he fired at him. I looked into the brush, knowing exactly where my deputy was sitting, and couldn't see anything indicating someone was there. I called out and had him put on an orange cap. The fluorescent color was partially visible, and that in itself would likely have prevented the shooting. But when my deputy donned a bright orange vest, it showed plainly through the heavy brush, and there was no doubt in my mind that if Fred had been wearing fluorescent orange clothing (as required by law) he would never have been shot.

In the end, Dick was prosecuted for shooting a human in mistake for wildlife, and Fred for failing to wear fluorescent orange clothing. I gave it a lot of thought before deciding to charge Fred for the violation considering how badly he was injured, but I couldn't help but feel he was partially to blame. Not only was he hunting someplace he wasn't supposed to be, but his failure to wear protective clothing most certainly contributed to the incident. Fred's fine was only twenty dollars, but Dick was looking at hundreds of dollars in fines and a lengthy revocation of his hunting and trapping privileges. There was also a potential lawsuit looming if Fred decided to pursue one. In the end, both men pled guilty and paid their fines, while learning a valuable lesson from their mistakes.

Controlled Hunts

Heavy deer populations confined to private parcels of land that were closed to hunting presented constant problems not only for me but for many of the people living in these areas. Because the deer had no natural predators and hunters had no access to these properties, there were hundreds of deer/vehicle crashes annually, resulting in roughly a quarter million dollars in damages per year. And this doesn't begin to include the emotional and physical damages suffered by people involved in the crashes. The deer were also destroying many of the shrubs, saplings and flowers growing on private properties throughout the county. I got a lot of complaints, but other than having controlled hunts on large properties in the vicinity, there was little I could do to help them. These were highly organized affairs held in areas closed to hunting that had become overrun with deer. Several come to mind, for most of them brought trouble for me in one way or another.

The Willow Grove Naval Air Station is exhibit one. This is a twelve hundred acre site, closed to hunting, that is secured by a six-foot chain link fence patrolled by armed guards. Outside the fence, it's surrounded by several large wooded tracts comprising thousands of additional acres. For heavily congested Montgomery County, this is a virtual wilderness, and because deer could easily jump over the six-foot fence into the air base to escape hunters and free roaming dogs on the outside, a burgeoning deer population developed within, thereby presenting some serious problems for the air base.

Because the air base was concerned about safety for the hundreds of men and women employed there and was bordered on one side by a heavily-traveled highway lined with commercial establishments, the government refused to allow hunting. But when aircraft started having problems with deer on the runways, with several planes striking them over the years, they soon saw the need for some kind of control effort, and I was contacted by telephone.

Because firearms were out of the question, I suggested having an organized hunt with bows and arrows only. There was no doubt we had more than enough bowhunters living in the area. All it would take was an advertisement in the local newspapers and we would have all the men we could handle. It didn't take long for the airbase to make up their minds, and I soon found myself coordinating the effort single-handedly. It was quite a task, but I worked with several military officers at the base to set up rotating hunts where men would drive deer into an area with bowhunters posted at the ready. Every safety precaution was taken. Everyone knew where the hunters were stationed and where the drivers would be coming in through the open woods. Hunters were clad in orange head-to-toe for precaution, and the operation turned out to be a huge success.

But it was short-lived.

Heavily populated metropolitan areas abound with bunny-huggers. And these people were calling me every day to complain about the hunt. When I politely tried to explain why it was necessary, they didn't want to hear it. Instead, they began contacting TV stations, radio commentators, newspapers and county commissioners complaining about the "evil" hunters killing all the deer and demanding that the government provide birth control pills for them! Imagine dealing with that kind of mentality. It plagued me all through my thirteen years in the county. And in the end, the anti-hunters won. The hunt was canceled, and the herd continued to grow. Years later, they brought in government marksmen to shoot the deer. And crazy as it might be, there were nowhere near the complaints, because this time local hunters weren't out there enjoying themselves. And that seemed to ease their concerns. Now it was mechanical. A sanitary, shoot-and-kill, military action.

Another incident that comes to mind was an organized hunt in Ridley Creek State Park. The park was overrun with deer because hunting wasn't allowed, and when they finally realized that the tremendous overpopulation of whitetails was over-browsing the forest understory and eating all their shrubs and flowers as well as having a dramatic negative effect on neighboring properties, they decided to cull the herd through an organized hunt with the aid of the Game Commission.

Although the state park and the Game Commission had gone through weeks of planning to make the hunt safe, the very first day was marred by a serious hunting accident. It was disheartening to say the least, and we couldn't help but question ourselves, wondering how we might have done things differently to help prevent it. I wrote about the incident in my book *Poacher Wars*, but it's worth a brief review here.

The incident was reported to me by a park ranger and I went directly to the scene, arriving before the medics got there. A young man was lying face up in a field. He was conscious but his breathing was shallow, and his condition grave. There was a perfectly round hole in his chest that came from a twelve-gauge shotgun loaded with buckshot.

I looked him in the eye. "Everything is going to be okay," I said.

He gazed at me for a moment, and then he blinked in mute response.

Because he was able to respond, I decided to ask him a few questions about the incident, telling him to blink once if his answer was yes and twice for no. I asked if he understood and he blinked once, so I knew it was a go.

I asked if he saw the person who shot him and he blinked once. That was a huge break in the case, and I suddenly had hope that I'd find the person. By asking just a few more questions, I was able to determine that the shooter was in his twenties, wearing a camo-orange vest and hat, and had a full beard.

As a result, I was able to stop the man at a guarded entryway as he attempted to leave the park in his pickup truck.

As it turned out, he had fired three shots at a fleeing deer while the victim was standing in an open field, fifty yards away, dressed in full orange. A single pellet (about twenty-four pellets in three rounds of double 0 buckshot) struck him in the chest. Instead of trying to help the wounded hunter, this coward chose to run away and leave him lying in the field to die. Fortunately, the paramedics arrived quickly and the man survived.

Tyler State Park in Bucks County was another organized hunt that I'll always remember. The park consists of seventeen-hundred acres and had an overabundance of deer that were eating everything in sight. I was assisting Game Warden Ed Bond on this one, and when we arrived at the entrance gate on a blistering cold December predawn morning, we were surprised to see a TV crew there. They were filming a dozen women as they sat on the cold macadam driveway blocking the hunters from entering the park. Ed Bond ordered them to move aside but they refused, so we called in the state police and park rangers for assistance. When they arrived, we picked up the women, one by one, and physically removed them from the entrance. One woman was well into her pregnancy, and I couldn't help but think about her unborn child, hoping there wouldn't be any complications as we carried her to the roadside.

Ed warned the protestors not to get in the way again or they would be charged with a fine for interfering with a lawful hunt. They stayed back, but once the hunters were registered and began posting themselves, the women formed into couples, locked arms, and started walking through the park hoping to chase the deer away from the hunters.

We couldn't arrest them for failing to wearing orange because they weren't hunting. And the park rangers couldn't arrest them for trespassing because the park was open to pedestrian travel. And although Ed Bond threatened to fine them for interference, without some overt action that prevented a hunter from pursuing his sport, there was no case.

And in truth, the women did more to help the hunters than hinder them as they tramped through the park clapping their hands and singing songs in an attempt to scare the deer away, the unintended consequence was that many hunters harvested a whitetail they otherwise wouldn't have seen. Thankfully, there were no injuries, and with the exception of the protestors, the hunt was deemed a huge success.

That was over forty years ago, and both state parks are still carrying on the tradition of an annual deer hunt, killing a hundred deer or more each year. Protestors continue to attend, spitting on hunters' cars, throwing nails into parking lots and causing general mayhem whenever they can, but the state police, park rangers and game wardens are used to it now and have well-planned strategies in place to handle any disorder that might arise.

Valley Forge National Park was another example of a deer herd explosion that had gone out of control. The 3500-acre park is the site of a Revolutionary War encampment northwest of Philadelphia and has over a million visitors each year. Washington's Headquarters, a stone house along the Schuylkill River, was occupied by George Washington from 1777 to 1778. Trails connect the key monuments and historic structures throughout the park, including the early-20th-century National Memorial Arch and the Muhlenberg Brigade's recreated log-cabin barracks. Deer roam about the park like cattle. They've grown accustomed to humans because they see people milling about every day. Joggers, hikers, bird watchers, picnickers, walking tours and bus tours are all part of a daily routine at the park.

It wasn't until 2009 that the park finally decided to do something about the overpopulation of deer. That was ten years after I transferred to Wyoming County in northeastern Pennsylvania. By then, the park had been so severely ravaged by over-browsing from the deer that habitat for a range of native wildlife species had been completely destroyed.

Something had to be done. The deer herd had grown to over 1200 whitetails (241 per square mile), and the goal was to reduce the population to a manageable level of less than 200 animals (31 per square mile, which is the state average) through controlled hunting.

Still, the anti-hunting sentiment was so strong that regulated and controlled hunting by sportsmen has never been implemented there. Instead, the park hires government sharpshooters to cull the herd each year.

Today the forest at the park is continuing to recover from decades of over-browsing, and park staff have documented native species seedlings that had not been present just a few years earlier.

Back in my days on patrol, there was only idle talk about controlling the herd. And with well over a thousand deer roaming the park—eight times the number found anywhere else in Pennsylvania—a number of unscrupulous hunters would attempt to sneak in during deer season. But the grounds were heavily patrolled by rangers, which made it extremely difficult for the would-be poachers to gain access—that is except for one, and his story begins on the following page.

Poacher Buddy Meyers

BUDDY MEYERS WAS NOT YOUR average poacher. I'd heard his name mentioned time and again by my former chief warden, Bill Locket, as well as my longtime friend, Warden Ed Bond. He'd never been arrested, not even for a minor game law violation. We knew he was poaching deer and had been for decades, but we could never catch him doing anything wrong. And much to our chagrin, he would parade through the county with a trophy-racked buck draped over the hood of his car every year, just to let us know he'd gotten away with his poaching antics one more time. To make matters worse, he lived less than a mile away from me. More than anything, I wanted to catch him poaching, but I'd settle for a minor violation too, just to get him on the books. Then one December day in 1986, a ranger from Valley Forge National Park contacted me about a man they caught hunting on posted property without permission. They said he also wasn't wearing fluorescent orange clothing as required under the Game Law. His name, they told me, was Buddy Meyers. What follows is a synopsis of how the case unfolded.

Deer season was in full swing as Ranger Troy Tomkins patrolled the outer limits of Valley Forge National Park on foot. It was a gorgeous afternoon with temperatures in the forties and a bright, sunny sky. Good day for a walk, he thought. Tomkins was concerned about the weight he'd gained over the recent holiday months, and the exercise would do him good. Besides, poachers could see him coming from a mile away in his marked patrol car. It restricted the territory he could cover, too. Foot patrol enabled him to reach places he couldn't get to by vehicle, and with reports of illegal hunting activity on the rise, he wanted to make the extra effort.

Tomkins was walking along the park boundary when he spotted a man standing by a cornfield belonging to Saint Gabriel's Hall, which was a shelter for homeless boys. He observed the individual through field glasses at approximately 150 yards. He was in his thirties wearing a tan colored cap, red and white plaid long-sleeve shirt, and a green vest over brown pants. He had dark hair and a mustache and was carrying a scoped shotgun.

Saint Gabriel's did not allow hunting on any of its property, so Tomkins used his portable radio to call for backup. He continued to observe the hunter and watched him shoulder his shotgun and "scope" him several times. Minutes later, a band of ten deer ran from the woods bordering the east side of the cornfield followed by a second group of thirteen deer on the westerly side. He continued to watch as a second man came out of a wooded area bordering the cornfield. He also carried a shotgun, and like the other, was not wearing any fluorescent orange clothing. This man was older, in his fifties with gray hair and wearing green clothing on his entire body. They met and had a brief conversation before walking along the woods edge away from Ranger Tomkins

As Tomkins continued to observe the hunters, two township police cars appeared. They came from opposite directions along an access road bordering the woods where the hunters were walking. But the men saw them from afar and ducked back into the trees were they couldn't be seen. The police officers were responding to the ranger's call for backup, but they never got out of their vehicles to search. Instead, they simply made a cursory drive-by and left the area, after which the men exited the woods and continued walking in a northerly direction until they were stopped by Ranger Cadman, who'd been called to the scene by Tomkins.

Cadman came at them from the south end of the cornfield. He was on foot and in full uniform when he approached the hunters. "Do you realize you're on private property?" he said.

The older man scoffed at him. "This ain't park property, so what's it to you?"

"I'm here as a courtesy for the neighboring property owners," he said. "Let's see some identification."

Both hunters showed him their IDs and he wrote down the information. The older man was Buddy Meyers, the other was Dennis Smith.

"This property is posted against hunting and trespassing," said Cadman. "Do you have permission to be here?"

Meyers shook his head in disgust. "I've been hunting here for thirty years! We used to have open land all around us. Now all we have is shopping centers, housing developments and city folks living here." He turned his head and spat. "No! I don't have permission to hunt here, but I know the man who farms this land, and he's being overrun with deer from *your* park. He can't hardly grow anything anymore, and now you want to harass us for trying to help him. You won't let us hunt on park property and you won't let us hunt here, even though the deer are taking over. There's so many of 'em they're like fleas on a dog's back!"

Ranger Cadman realized the man had a valid point. He was a hunter himself and would love to see the national park open for hunting. But he had a job to do, and because he had no jurisdiction on private property, he forwarded the information about trespassing to the local police and telephoned the Game Commission about the blaze orange violation that same day.

When the dispatcher called me about Buddy Meyers, my heart skipped a beat. Just knowing where that man was on any given day during hunting season was a gift in itself. Although I was surprised to learn he'd been stopped by the rangers, I wasn't surprised to hear he was trespassing and even less surprised that he wasn't wearing orange. He'd be a fool to trespass on posted property wearing clothes that exposed him so readily. Meyers was a known poacher, and he was good at it. He hunted anyplace he wanted, whenever he wanted. He had little concern for seasons, bag limits or other game laws. He was a consummate outlaw who always managed to slip away unscathed. Now he'd been caught. A minor violation as far at the twenty-dollar fine was concerned, but he'd finally be on the books.

Because it was well into deer season, with only a few days remaining, I suspected Buddy Meyers had already killed a deer, if not several. I was disappointed that the rangers hadn't checked his or Smith's hunting licenses to see if their deer tags had been used. Because Montgomery County was in the Special Regulations Area (buckshot and archery only for deer), the statewide two-week bucks-only season didn't apply. Here hunters could kill a buck or a doe during the entire two weeks, provided they had an antlerless deer license in addition to their regular hunting license.

Thinking the men might still be in the area, I headed for the national park hoping to find them. As usual, traffic was heavy, and because I was in the opposite end of the county, it took more than forty minutes to get there. After meeting with Rangers Tomkins and Cadman for a brief rundown of what happened earlier, I drove out to the cornfield where Meyers and Smith had been hunting. Ranger Tomkins told me he'd been getting reports of shots fired in that area for the past several days, which is why he went off national park property to look around.

In a way, I was surprised to learn this. Although I considered him a fine lawman and appreciated his dedication to the agency he worked for, I had to shake my head about his concern over hunting on neighboring properties. The park was overrun with deer. They were destroying the forested understory and causing collisions with motorists in the area. He'd seen twenty-three deer run from the woods where Meyers and Smith were hunting. And that was a small fraction of the thousand or more whitetails inhabiting the 3,500-acre park. On the other hand, I was grateful for his willingness to go above and beyond the call of duty. Had he not, one of the biggest poachers in the county would have gotten away scot free. Tomkins and Cadman were both willing to testify in court against the men, so I planned to file charges for hunting without orange clothing later that day, but first I wanted to head out to the wooded area they'd been hunting to see what I found.

I began my search by walking the edge of the woods where the two men had been stopped. The woodlot wasn't all that large, maybe twenty acres or so, and when I got halfway to the end of the tree line, I spotted something shiny lying in the grass by a large sweet gum tree. A candy bar wrapper! Snickers, one of my favorites, and when my stomach growled at the sight of it, I suddenly remembered that I'd missed lunch. I've always had to eat like a shrew to keep from losing weight, and had packed two sandwiches before starting my patrol that day, but it was getting late. *Looks like I'll be having lunch for dinner*, I thought. The candy wrapper had to be from Buddy Meyers. It was just like him to throw it on the ground rather than put it in his pocket. But his slovenly nature was about to be his downfall, for it gave me a starting point to begin my search.

I entered the trees at that point and circled the woods, gradually working my way toward the center. After making several loops, my suspicions were confirmed. Two dead deer, both does, lay on the forest floor under a pile of dead leaves. Both had been killed with buckshot at close range, not far from where they lay. They'd been gutted, their entrails dumped in piles several feet away. A pair of cheap latex gloves lay next to them. It was no wonder the rangers didn't expect they'd killed anything. The gloves ensured there'd be no blood on their hands and the deer had been concealed so that a brief observation would reveal nothing. There was no way to prove Meyers and Smith had anything to do with the killings. They'd left no telltale evidence behind, no ejected shotgun shells for the crime lab to link markings on the primers to the firing pins of their shotguns. I didn't bother examining the carcasses for shotgun pellets either, since there was no chance of matching any pellets found in their bodies to a gun. Unlike bullets, where grooves on the projectile can be matched to the rifling inside a gun barrel, shotguns are smoothbore and don't leave markings.

There was no doubt in my mind that Meyers and his friend planned to come back after dark for the deer. The sun would set in less than an hour, so I hustled over to my patrol car and drove back to the national park. After making arrangements with Ranger Tomkins to leave my car overnight in an inconspicuous location, I wolfed down two ham and cheese sandwiches, grabbed a thermos of hot coffee and a wool blanket, and hotfooted it back into the woods. I intended to wait for them there, even if it took all night.

But sometimes the best laid plans go awry. And by two o'clock in the morning, I was beginning to rethink my idea of a long night in the woods as the cold December air began to take its toll. Fighting the urge to go home and lie in a warm bed, I pulled the earflaps down on my faux sealskin patrol cap, draped the wool blanket around me and looked up at the sky. A gazillion stars danced like sparkling diamonds in an endless black abyss, and it brought me peace as I gazed upon God's grand creation. Such divine beauty could never have come from happenstance, I reasoned. I stepped back and sat on the pile of dead leaves I'd stacked earlier. Leaning back against a lofty pine, I squeaked open the lid on my Stanley thermos and poured. There's nothing like the hearty aroma a hot cup of black coffee brings on a cold winter's night, I thought. Whiffs of gray steam swirled from the mouth of my thermos as the silky liquid gurgled into the stainless steel lid that served as a cup. I held it in my hands, warming them, sipping slowly on the robust Arabian brew, and suddenly all seemed right in the world.

It was a Saturday night, and I started thinking about my side job at a local nightclub. When a friend at the gym where I trained each day told me they were looking for a doorman at the club where he worked, and the pay was twenty-five dollars cash for one night's work—enough to keep gas in my car for a month—I immediately applied and was hired. The extra money came in handy. A game warden's salary wasn't much to talk about in those days, especially with a wife and a five-year-old at home. Because most of my Game Commission work occurred during the day, with animal complaints, roadkilled deer and general hunting violations, I only worked one night per week so it wouldn't interfere. I would lose that extra income tonight.

A doorman is a gracious term for a bouncer. The nightclub served alcohol and had live entertainment on Friday and Saturday nights. It was a rock and roll bar with a large dance floor that could hold more than a hundred customers. The music was so loud that you could feel vibrations in the walls from the pulsating blare of two floorstanding speakers set up by the musicians. I had to plug my ears with cotton to keep from getting a headache. The patrons were often rowdy, especially when drinking excessively, which was common. Drug use was rampant, including heroin, cocaine and other hallucinogens. My job, along with several other men, was to check IDs on every person at the door to make sure they were of legal age and to remove disruptive or disorderly customers, which generally meant physically extracting them from the bar and escorting them out the front door. Because fights would break out at times, we all watched out for each other, and I worried that my absence tonight might result in a doorman being harmed.

I never told my supervisor about the side job because I was afraid he wouldn't allow it. Back then, the Game Commission owned you. A game warden couldn't leave his assigned district, not even to go shopping, without permission from his supervisor. You were expected to be on call twenty-four hours per day, even though you were only paid for eight. In retrospect, it was bad thinking on my part to work at the club. If I would have been injured by a customer, it could have kept me out of work for weeks or months. And if I injured someone that had to be removed from the premises, I could have been in deep trouble. Considering what was going on there every night, the chances were high that someone would eventually be hurt.

Thoughts about the nightclub raced through my mind as I took one last sip of coffee and screwed the lid back on my thermos. Maybe I should stop working there, I thought. Just last week I had two altercations that could have ended bad.

One was a bar fight where two men were scrapping on the ground. I bent over the man on top to pick him up when he snapped his head back and bloodied my nose. I quickly put him in a full nelson and lifted him off the other guy. As I carried him toward the door, another bouncer saw me bleeding and rushed over to assist. My friend got a little too excited about my bloody nose, and the poor fellow went out the door literally flying through the air. Not good. Later, when we were closing up the place at two in the morning, there was a small group who refused to leave. When I insisted they had to go, one of the men came at me and I had to physically subdue him. Again, not good. A number of other incidents were recalled as I sat by the tree, and I began having serious doubts about the job. I closed my eyes for a moment as they rolled through my mind, and within seconds I fell fast asleep...

CAW-CAW-CAW!

I awoke in a flash. It was daybreak, the branches above me occupied by dozens of crows, their shiny black eyes focused on the two dead deer. As I started to get to my feet the crows flew off in a cacophony of squawks and raspy cries of alarm. My legs were numb from the cold and lack of movement. I rubbed them with icy hands for several minutes before easing myself off the frozen ground. I'd never felt so stiff in my entire life. And as I hobbled out of the woods toward my patrol car, I shook my head in despair. Buddy Meyers was too smart to take the risk. He suspected the rangers would contact me and decided not to return for the deer. No wonder he'd earned the status of a legendary poacher. There was no way he'd ever admit killing the deer, so all I could do at this point was file charges against him for the blaze orange violation. But I didn't know anything about his friend, Dennis Smith. Perhaps there was a chance I could bluff him into a confession. It was my only hope, so my next step was to pay him a visit.

By the time I got back to my patrol car, my blood had circulated enough so that my feet didn't feel like blocks of ice. I slid inside, started the engine, and turned the heat on full blast. I sat there for a while, warming my body before dropping the car into gear and driving down to the woods for the deer. I dragged both carcasses out, loaded them on my big game carrier, and dropped them off with two needy families in the area. Then it was home to say hello to my family, a quick shower and off to church. When services were over, we stopped at a favorite restaurant for a bite to eat. Our Sunday ritual. Maryann wasn't too happy about my returning to work that day, but I explained that I needed to find Dennis Smith and question him while the case was still fresh. She smiled and wished me well. Her life was as hectic as mine. Raising children is one of the most difficult and time-consuming tasks anyone could ever have, and I respected her for the wonderful job she was doing with our son, Jesse.

Dennis Smith was home when I knocked on the door. My patrol car was parked in plain view of the picture window at the front of the house. I wanted him to see it. Wanted him to sweat it out a little. Sometimes an outlaw will be so panicky at the sight of the warden's car that by the time they work up the nerve to answer the door, they've already convinced themselves to give up. Not in Smith's case, however.

He was thirty-three years old, handsome, brash and cocky. Smith stood lean and tall: six-foot-two with broad shoulders, wavy black hair, and a thick mustache that made him look like Tom Selleck. He wore jeans and a denim shirt untucked as he leaned against the door jam and frowned at me. "This about yesterday?" he asked.

"That's right," I told him.

He shrugged dismissively. "We gave the rangers our IDs. Told 'em we had permission to hunt there. What more do they want from us?"

"The rangers told me you and Buddy Meyers *didn't* have permission, that you were trespassing. But I'm not here to dispute that. I found two dead deer back in the woods. I know you were involved. I can make things a lot easier on you if you cooperate with me."

Smith nodded reflectively and folded his arms across his chest. "Hmmm. How's that?"

"There are a number of violations you could be charged with," I said. "I can reduce them substantially. The potential loss of your hunting privileges could also be eliminated. Interested?"

"Depends on what you're asking for?"

"The truth," I said. "All I want is for you to tell me the truth about the deer."

Smith looked at me for a long time. Then the corners of his eyes wrinkled in mirth and a broad smile crossed his face. "What deer?"

There was something about the man that made me cringe. I could feel it all around me. Some wicked and terrible presence that seemed to flow from within his soul. He'd done bad things in his life. Things that were far worse than poaching deer. Dreadful things. Don't ask me how I knew. I couldn't tell you. I'm not a fortune teller. But there are times when things come to me. They always come true. I can't summon them, but it does happen occasionally, and only when I'm not expecting it. This was one of those times.

Dennis Smith wanted to have fun with me. Play me along. I had nothing on him and he knew it. My bluff fell flat and I had to turn around and walk away. It was difficult for me to do that. I hate to lose, especially when I know I'm right. Smith and Meyers had killed those deer and they were going to get away with it. And no matter how much that bothered me, I couldn't do a thing about it. Game wardens don't always come out on top. We have huge districts to patrol; the average is four hundred square miles, sometimes more. And with over a million hunters in Pennsylvania, it was impossible for 120 state game wardens to weed out the bad ones and bring them to justice every time they violated the law. But on the flip side, Meyers and Smith weren't getting away with everything. I had them rock solid for hunting without orange, and they were likely to pay fines for trespassing as well, but that would be up to the local police. Game wardens in Pennsylvania do not enforce trespassing laws.

I filed citations against both men later that week. Dennis Smith checked off a guilty plea on the back of the citation and paid his fine through the mail. Buddy Meyers requested a hearing before the local district justice. I couldn't believe it. I had two park rangers who saw him hunting while dressed entirely in green. Ranger Tomkins observed him from afar, but Ranger Cadman stood face to face with Meyers when he stopped him in the field to question him about hunting on private property. He requested identification and Meyers presented it to him. How in the world did Buddy Meyers think he was going to get away with this one?

I was about to find out.

It took three months before his case came up in court. I couldn't help but wonder if he'd even show up. If not, there would be a trial in absentia (in his absence), he would be found guilty, and a warrant issued for his arrest. This is what I expected would happen. He'd play around, duck and hide, then pay his fine once I caught up to him with a warrant in my hand. But to my surprise, when I walked into the courtroom with Tomkins and Cadman, Buddy Meyers was sitting in a chair waiting for us.

I had never laid eyes on him before. Meyers was like a ghost. I'd heard rumors about him for years, but never actually met the man. He was twice my age—pushing sixty with gray hair, a thick, protruding forehead, and dark eyes that could look right through you. A rugged man with a barrel chest and powerful shoulders, he conveyed the appearance of someone who could swing a dead deer over his shoulders and carry it out of the woods on the run.

In trials, the prosecutor always lays out his case first, followed by cross-examination from the defendant or his attorney. Meyers didn't have an attorney, and it would be up to him to shed doubt on anything my witnesses had to say. The trial wouldn't be difficult. I had two national park rangers who were credible eyewitnesses to the crime. I started with Ranger Tomkins as my first witness, and after being sworn in, he took a seat alongside the judge and described in detail how he'd watched Meyers hunting deer on private property without wearing any fluorescent orange material as required by law. Instead, he was dressed entirely in green. Although he had seen him from afar, Tomkins had been using powerful field glasses and was able to point his finger directly at Buddy Meyers confirming that he was the same man he'd seen that day in the field.

My next witness was Ranger Cadman, who testified that he'd been called to assist Ranger Tomkins and when he walked along the woodlot in search of two hunters, he encountered Buddy Meyers and Dennis Smith. He testified that both men were carrying shotguns and had hunting licenses; both men admitted hunting for deer on posted property without permission; and neither of them wore any orange clothing. Cadman looked over at Meyers, pointed directly at him and said, "That is the man I saw that day. And when I asked for identification he produced a driver's license with the name Buddy Meyers printed on it."

I was my own last witness for the trial. And although I wasn't prosecuting Meyers for killing a deer, I wanted to inject that part of my investigation into the case. I explained to the judge how I'd gone back there later in the day and came upon two dead deer that had been recently killed. Both had been gutted and covered with leaves to conceal them. I explained that Meyers and Smith had been observed in and around the wooded area where the deer were hidden, and that they were the only hunters that the rangers encountered that day. The judge listened intently to my testimony, glancing over at Meyers now and then as I spoke. But because I hadn't brought charges against him for killing the deer, I didn't know if my testimony would carry any weight in the judge's final verdict.

I rested my case. There was no need to say any more. I had him rock solid. It was his turn to take the stand, and I couldn't wait to hear how he'd try to weasel out of this one.

Buddy Meyers raised his right hand and swore before the judge that he would tell the truth, the whole truth, and nothing but the truth. Then he sat in a witness chair to her left and proceeded to tell anything but the truth. According to Meyers, he wasn't hunting when he was stopped by the rangers, claiming that he was cutting across the cornfield on his way back to his truck because he'd forgotten to put on his orange vest. He said he had an orange hat in his back pocket but the ranger never asked to see it. He insisted that he was completely innocent, and if Wasserman had bothered to interview him later that day, or any day before the trial, he would have told him the same thing. Then he pointed a finger at me shook his head in contempt. "He could have saved us all a lot of time and energy, but he failed to do his job by not talking to me first to hear my side of the story!"

I had to give him credit for a great tale: turn the tables on the warden and blame him for your misdeed. No wonder the guy was a legend in his own time. But the judge wasn't buying it and found him guilty. The fine was twenty dollars. Court costs were twenty-three-fifty. And I couldn't have been happier that he'd gone down for double his initial cost due to his dishonest testimony.

Buddy Meyers stormed out of the courtroom after paying his fine and waited for me in the parking lot where I'd left my patrol car. "Good job, warden," he said as I walked toward my car. "First time I ever had to pay a fine to the Game Commission."

"Why did you tell the judge you were going back to get your orange vest?" I said. "You knew that wasn't true."

"That's right," he said. "I lied! What did you expect me to do?"

I stared at him in utter disbelief. How do you answer a question like that? I'd heard plenty of lies and phony alibis from poachers before, but this was the first time someone had actually admitted to my face that he'd lied in court, that he'd given false testimony and perjured himself. And I suddenly knew why Buddy Meyers chose Dennis Smith for a friend. The two were exactly the same: sociopaths in my opinion…men who took what they wanted, whenever they wanted, at the expense of anyone who stood in their way.

I had nothing more to say to him, so I walked over to my patrol, slid inside and drove off without a glance his way. I never ran into Buddy Meyers after that day. I'm sure he was out there poaching deer at every opportunity, but with three districts under my care, generating hundreds of roadkilled deer and thousands of nuisance wildlife complaints, it was virtually impossible for me to focus on any individual outlaw for any significant length of time, either in or out of the hunting season. Hence, I put the incident aside and focused on my daily responsibilities. I tried not to dwell on unresolved cases. We don't always get our man, and I knew I could live with that as long as I had done my best to bring an outlaw to justice.

Slaughter of Innocents

THE CANADA GOOSE WAS OFTEN public enemy number one for anyone with a lake, pond or waterway in Montgomery County. One of the biggest complaints about these large birds was the amount of dung they left behind. Sometimes there were so many geese inhabiting a relatively small pond that the water would become polluted from all their feces. And because they were grass eaters, they would often walk from a pond or stream onto nearby private lawns to peck away at the grass for hours, causing extensive damage to otherwise pristine lawns. This was especially true on golf courses where the greens are manicured to perfection. Another concern for many folks was their aggressive nature during nesting season. I received a number of complaints each year about Canada geese chasing after people that came too close to their nests. How close is too close? That was up to the geese, and for some of these birds, anyone within fifty yards of a nest would be targeted. People were getting hurt sometimes, too. I had several incidents were bicyclists lost control of their wheels and crashed after being ambushed by an angry goose, while people on foot would be bitten hard enough to leave black and blue marks on bare legs. I wrote earlier about our annual goose roundups, and between that and all the other problems they created, I was not a fan of the Canada goose.

But when I got a report about someone shooting them inside a township park, I could feel the hair on the back of my neck bristle. I happened to be in the area trying to locate a roadkilled deer reported by the Abington Police Department, and when I called for a better location, I was informed that the officer who could help me was searching for someone who shot a bunch of geese and left them lying along the Pennypack Creek in Lorimar Park. It was eleven o'clock in the morning on a Wednesday in June 1981. And it was at a time when the geese were raising their young. No one in their right mind could mistake the park for anything but what it was: a manicured area of land, left in its natural state for the enjoyment of the public. The place was frequently visited by families. Women often strolled along the rolling macadam walkways holding hands with their children. There were swings and playgrounds and picnic benches situated throughout the property. Who would do something like that?

It wasn't a surprise that the police hadn't bothered to contact me. And had I not called them about the deer I was trying to locate, I may never have known about the killings. That's the way things worked in the heavily populated suburban townships under my jurisdiction. The police were usually first on the scene of a game law violation, and would start an investigation without ever thinking to call the Game Commission.

Fortunately, I was close by, so I drove directly to the park and started my investigation. Because the grass was still wet from the morning's rain, I could see the impression of footprints from several individuals along the streambank. One had to be the suspect, the others most likely came from the police. I soon came upon a dead Canada goose at the water's edge. Kneeling by it, I found a single bullet hole in its chest from a small caliber firearm, likely a .22. I continued along the stream and found a total of eight dead geese shot at random. Three were goslings, one being only eight inches tall. It was sickening to see their bodies scattered about the park like so much refuse.

I began photographing the scene for evidence when a police officer approached.

"Our dispatcher said you were on your way," he said. "Thought I'd come find you."

We shook hands. "I realize you have a number of local laws that were broken here," I said, "but this is also a serious Game Law violation, not to mention the federal implications."

"Federal?" he said with a raised brow.

"Canada geese are protected by the United States Fish and Wildlife Service," I told him. "Whoever did this is looking at some serious state and federal fines."

"Good to hear," he replied. "One of our men was able to track the suspect to within twenty-five feet of a home just outside the park. We're heading over there right now. Where's your car?"

I told him it was at the park entrance and he said he'd meet me there and take me to the suspect's house.

I hustled back to my patrol car and found the police officer already waiting for me in a marked vehicle. I got inside my sedan and started the engine. The policeman switched on his emergency lights and stepped on it, his tires burning rubber on the macadam road as he tore out of the parking lot. I decked the accelerator and stayed close behind. In minutes we were there: three Abington police cars, two Lorimar Park cars and my own state vehicle lined up in front of the suspect's house.

At the sight of so many lawmen, the average person might have thought we were looking for a murder suspect. But this was city life, where a man shooting at geese is considered armed and dangerous—a threat not only to the general public but also to the police officers who go after him. Actually, it's not a bad assumption to make, because you never really know. An armed man with no criminal record can be just as dangerous as a convicted felon. I thought about the hundreds of armed hunters I'd approached over the years without backup. While most hunters are good people, you never knew when someone with a loaded gun in their hands might have a serious criminal background…or be mentally unstable. It was in that very township, just the summer before, that a father took his young son for a walk in the woods. Tragically, the outing resulted in a murder/suicide. When I heard about it on the news, I suddenly realized how potentially dangerous a game warden's job can be. For had I been called to investigate what appeared to be a simple case of hunting without orange clothing, I might have been killed too, for there was no way I would have suspected the man's deadly intentions.

I gathered the other police officers together and explained that this was a matter for the Game Commission, rather than local authorities, clarifying that they would also be able to file charges against him, but the initial investigation belonged to me. They didn't have a problem with that, and offered their services as backup while I took over the case. I was glad to have them along.

I knocked on the suspect's door and was greeted by a man in his late forties. He wore Ben Franklin glasses over a kindly face that gave him look of an intellectual.

"State Game Commission," I said. "I'm here concerning some geese that were shot."

He looked over my shoulder at all the police cars, and I could almost hear the cogs turning in his brain as he tried to sort out what was happening. It was the look of stunned innocence, and I knew that it was someone else who had been tracked to the house.

"I don't own a gun, officer, and I'd never kill a harmless animal." He paused, then looked up and down the street. "My neighbors are going to think something terrible happened here. Please go now."

"Someone shot eight geese back at the park," I said. "The police tracked the suspect to your house." His eyes suddenly grew wide as things started falling into place: the park, the dead geese, the suspect tracked to his house…he knew who was responsible and why I was standing at his door.

"I've been home all day," he said, feigning innocence. "I told you I didn't shoot any geese."

He was covering for someone. He never opened the door more than halfway, using it as a shield as we spoke.

"Mind if I step inside?" I asked.

He closed the door a few inches more and shook his head. "This isn't a good time. I'm busy with paperwork."

"Sir, I have enough probable cause for a search warrant. If you close the door, that's what I'm going to have in my hand the next time you see me." I looked at my wristwatch. "The judge's office is a mile away. It'll take me less than an hour to return with one. Then I'm going to go through your entire house, garage, cars and anyplace else that I think might be hiding a rifle or handgun. Does that sound like something you'd want?"

He shook his head no.

"Then open the door and let's talk."

He looked at the police cars again and stepped back. "Come in."

It was a spacious two story colonial dating back to the last century. The planked hardwood floors were refinished beautifully. Three-piece oak crown molding adorned every ceiling; a long staircase leading to the second floor was decorated in a heavy, ornate wood pattern; the walls covered in a traditional wainscot of richly layered wood panels. It didn't look like a place that would harbor someone who shot a bunch of harmless geese just to watch them die.

"I'm officer Wasserman. Your name, sir?"

"Bart Hanson," he said. "Look, I'm a little shook up over this whole thing. First I see an army of police outside my door and then you threaten me with a search warrant over some geese that were shot in the park. I told you I was here all day." He pointed to a desk stacked with folders. "Take a look for yourself. I've got a weeks' worth of papers to go through for my business."

"The sooner we get this over with, the sooner you can get back to work." I said. "We know the person who shot the geese came from this house. I don't think it was you. All I want is a little cooperation so we can all put this situation to rest."

Hanson sighed. "I *am* cooperating. That's why I let you in."

"Do you live alone?"

He shook his head no.

"Kids?"

"I have a son. He's twenty."

"Is he here today?"

"No, just me."

"I'd like to talk to him. Where is he?"

"He lives with his mother," he said. "About two miles from here."

I was sure Hanson knew his son killed the geese and that he was trying to protect him. I decided to put more pressure on him, force his hand. Turning abruptly, I walked to the door and opened it.

"Where are you going?"

I turned and faced him. "I don't have the time to stand here while you beat around the bush pretending you don't know anything. I'm going to get a search warrant. But first I'm going to have the police surround your house to make sure you don't try to leave or tamper with any evidence."

He raised his hands in a gesture of submission. "Whoa! Don't do that! My neighbors will be talking about this for years!"

I stepped back and closed the door. "I want to see your son right now," I warned. "Otherwise—"

"Okay. I'll get him. Just trust me for a moment. Let me go to his mother's house and bring him back. It's only a ten minute drive."

"I'll go with you."

"No. Please. It's best for everyone if I do it alone. I need to talk to him. Ease him into this. If he sees you with me, he'll run out the back door and hide. I give you my word. I *will* bring him back here for you."

"Agreed," I said. But I'm going to search your car for any guns before you go."

"Understood. But can you ask the other officers to leave? It would be better if they weren't here when we return."

I didn't have much of a choice. The last thing I wanted to do was run to the judge for a search warrant. I told Hanson earlier that it would take less than an hour to get one, made it sound simple, but I knew it would take a lot longer. In truth, I'd spend the rest of the afternoon chasing down the judge and the district attorney before I could return with the warrant. I believed Hanson was sincere in his offer to bring back his son, so I took the risk and asked the other officers to vacate. Told them everything was settled and that I'd stop by later with a report for them.

Hanson's son looked just like his dad: a young man in his early twenties, he was tall with a lanky build and wore round, wire-rimmed glasses. I waited over an hour for them to return, and when I saw Hanson's Mercedes-Benz pull into the driveway, I breathed a sigh of relief.

"Let's talk inside," said Hanson as he and his son walked over to meet me by my patrol car. His son gawked at me through thick-lensed glasses and said nothing. In most cases, I would have insisted that the suspect sit in my patrol car, alone, for an interrogation, but I had a feeling things might go better if Hanson's son spoke to me in the comfort of familiar surroundings, so I grabbed a citation pad from inside my car and trailed them into the house.

"Coffee?" asked Hanson as we stepped into the kitchen and sat at a spacious round table.

I shook my head no.

"Thank you for cooperating with me," he said.

I took a notepad and pen from my shirt pocket and set it on the table. "I expect the same from you and your son."

He nodded in agreement.

I turned to his son. "Your name?"

"Francis Hanson," he said. Then he looked at his father with stubborn eyes.

"Go ahead, son," insisted his father. "Tell the officer what happened. I gave him my word."

He shrugged indifferently. "I did it," he said. "Okay?"

"Did what?"

"I shot all the geese. That's what you're here for, isn't it?"

"What did you shoot them with?"

"A .22 rifle."

"Where is it?"

"I don't remember."

"Francis!" his father scolded "Stop this nonsense and tell the man where you put your gun!"

Francis rolled his eyes. "It's upstairs, under my bed. Okay?"

His father rose from his chair. "I'll go get it for you, officer."

"Best if you don't touch it," I said. "I'll get it later."

He nodded understandingly and sat down.

"Why did you shoot all the geese," I asked. "Three were just goslings."

"Goslings?"

"Baby geese."

He leaned back in his chair, folded his arms and grinned at me. "Big or small, they all had to fall."

"Why?" I asked again. "What was the purpose? Were they just target practice or do you simply enjoy killing things?"

He shrugged. "I was bored, that's all."

I said, "So that was your plan from the beginning: bring a rifle into the park and just start shooting the geese for target practice, right?"

"Not really," he said. "I carry a gun everywhere I go because of this mental problem I have. The geese just happened to be there. I didn't plan anything, it was more like a spontaneous thing."

I didn't know if he was serious or just being a smart aleck, but I did know I'd had enough of him for the day. I went upstairs with his father and retrieved a .22 caliber, Model 20 Squires Bingham rifle from under a bed. After securing it in my patrol car, I went back to the park and gathered up all the dead geese. One of them, a large gander, had been shot multiple times. I removed one of the bullets from its chest and put it into a plastic bag for ballistics evidence, then I disposed of the carcasses at a rendering plant in the northern part of the county.

Later that day, I filed citations against Francis Hanson for killing eight Canada geese in closed season, using a semi-automatic rifle to hunt, wanton waste, violating the Duck Stamp Act, using a rifle in the Special Regulations Area, and using a rifle to kill migratory waterfowl. He pled guilty to all charges, paid a thousand dollars in fines (actually, his father paid, but I had no control over that) and received a ten year suspension of his hunting and trapping privileges.

Of all the investigations I conducted over more than three decades in the field, I only ran into one other person like Francis Hanson, and that story is next. Regarding Hanson, I do believe he was mentally unstable and can only hope that his father got him the medical attention he needed to help him become a healthy and rational human being.

Mad Bobby Clark

SEVENTEEN-YEAR-OLD BOBBY CLARK took the shotgun he got for his birthday and drove his daddy's brand new Chevy to the edge of a cornfield a few miles from home. It was a Saturday afternoon. His pockets bulged with fresh ammo as he carried a burlap bag heavy with dove decoys into the field. He was going to shoot some doves, lots of doves he hoped. He also hoped that the wild-haired old lady who lived in a house at the edge of the field didn't come after him again. He was getting tired of her. She'd chase off the doves every time she came storming out the back door. He'd have to do something about her one of these days. Yep. Her time was coming, and today just might be the day.

Bobby Clark was an immature spoiled brat who was given everything he wanted by his parents. They promised him a new car of his own for a graduation present at the end of the school year. Something nice that he could use to drive back and forth to college. He was in twelfth grade and loving every minute of his last year in high school. And why not? Bobby was a track star and a straight A student. He had a lot of friends in school and all the teachers liked him.

But Bobby had a temper that was difficult to control. He kept it hidden from his teachers and his track coach, but some of his friends at school had seen him lose it when things didn't go his way, and it wasn't pretty. In fact, it was a bit frightening. It wouldn't take much to set him off, either. Take the kid who cut in front of him on the way into the lavatory one day. As they stood side-by-side at the flushable wall fixtures, his neighbor soon discovered Bobby's flow pelting his shoe.

"Hey-hey-hey!" he yelped, quickly backing away.

"Sorry about that," Bobby replied coolly. "Better clean yourself up or you'll be late for class."

As long as things were going his way, Bobby was fine. And most days things did go his way. He was intellectually gifted, so classes were a breeze. And he was a natural athlete, which often put him at the top of the heap in school sports. But because everything came so easily for him, he never learned how to deal with adversity. It was always his way or the highway. In other words, Bobby was emotionally unstable, which was often displayed by the irrational relationships he had with people he didn't like as well as his unpredictable reaction toward difficult situations.

But when Bobby was hunting, he was at peace with the world, for he was in complete control. He was the alpha male of his universe, a super predator, the one who chose life or death for all things that came under his gun.

His heart thrummed in his chest as he picked a spot at the center of the standing corn and stepped into the first row to conceal himself. He was dressed entirely in camouflage, head to toe, and he was the only hunter in the entire fifty-acre field. There was a small farm pond close by where the doves loved to congregate. His decoys would surely lure them in. Yes, it was going to be a very good day, he thought. A very good day indeed.

It was late; the sun would set in two hours, so Bobby hunkered down and waited for the birds to start flying in. As he did, his mind drifted back. It was only a week ago when Crazy Lady came charging out of her house screaming bloody murder about all the shooting he was doing. It was the second time she'd done this in so many weeks. Bobby was a crack shot. He never missed. And he'd been able to kill a half dozen birds before she showed. Maybe he'd luck out today and she'd be out shopping or visiting somebody. Bobby intended to make up for lost birds on account of her. His plan was to keep shooting until he had a burlap bag full of doves. The way he figured it, she owed him twelve birds: six each day for the two days he had to stop shooting, after which he'd take his daily limit of twelve doves for today's hunt.

For her sake, he hoped Crazy Lady wasn't home, and if she was, she'd better stay put. Because this time he wasn't walking away. This time he was gonna show her who was boss. He racked a fresh shell into the chamber of his pump gun as the first dove tested the field. *Come and get it!* he whispered. And as the rest of the flock rocketed overhead, Bobby let loose his wrath.

*B*oom! *Boom-boom-boom!*

Maggie shook her head with dismay. He was back! Had to be him. Nobody else would be so inconsiderate. He'd been at it for almost an hour, and every time she thought about going out there, the shooting would stop. Then ten or fifteen minutes would pass and it would start again. He was a teenaged boy, too young to be hunting alone as far as she was concerned. She'd confronted him twice before, and although he always left when she scolded him, he became more resistant each time. Last Saturday was the worst. The kid insisted that he had permission to hunt in the field and refused to leave. Maggie told him she didn't care if he hunted in the field; she just wanted him to go farther away from her house.

"But this is the best spot!" he complained. "And you got no right to hassle me like this."

"You're in a safety zone," she declared. "I asked a friend who hunts and he told me you have to be more than 150 yards from my house."

"But I'm not shooting toward your house!" he said angrily.

"You still aren't supposed to be this close," insisted Maggie. "I'm trying to work with you, son. Don't you understand?"

Bobby Clark clenched his jaw tight and stared at her for a long moment. "What did you call me?" he said angrily. His voice was acid.

Maggie stepped back. Something in his face had changed, as if a dark cloud had passed over him. But there was no cloud. "I...I didn't call you anything."

"You called me son!" he shrieked. "You have no right! I'm not your son and you're not my mother!" His entire being began to shake. Eyes boring into her, lips twisting into an ugly scowl.

Maggie's heart began to pound. "I didn't mean to suggest anything like that. Just go farther from my house and hunt. That's all I ask. Now please leave before I have to call the police."

Police! Her threat suddenly brought him to his senses. The last thing he needed was the cops coming after him because Crazy Lady had nothing better to do than harass him. And so he took the doves he'd killed, packed up his decoys, and left the field entirely.

But later that day, he started thinking about the situation.

And the more he did, the angrier he got.

The following Saturday, Bobby Clark returned to the cornfield behind Maggie's house and set up in the same spot as before. No way was he gonna let Crazy Lady tell him what to do. It wasn't long before the doves began winging overhead, and Bobby let them have it!

Boom! Boom-boom!

Maggie heard the shots from inside her house and knew it was him again. He was calling her. Daring her to do something about it. She remembered what happened the last time she confronted him. The way he turned. The way she suddenly feared him. Maggie lived alone and always took care of herself. She depended on no one, working nights as a waitress while spending her weekdays cleaning houses. She considered herself a strong and independent woman. How could she let a teenaged boy intimidate her like that? And here he was again, shooting up a storm. She thought about calling the police, but it might be an hour before they arrived and she was having none of it.

Maggie was a stout and powerful woman. Enraged by his taunting, she stormed out the back door waving her hands and shouting warnings to a flock of doves sailing overhead. They scattered like arrows in the wind, safe from the hunter's gun.

She marched toward the cornfield, hands clenched into fists as she rounded the corner of the field, feet pounding the earth, eyes locked on Bobby Clark as he stood before her.

"I have had it with you!" she shouted. "Pack your gear and get out!"

Bobby stood post straight as she came at him. "My gun is loaded!" he warned. "You better watch out!"

Maggie's heart was pounding through her chest. She saw red. Nothing he said could have frightened her. He'd have to shoot her dead to stop her. In seconds she was nose to nose with him, her breathing labored from the adrenalin rush surging through her veins.

"Get away from me!" shouted Bobby. He held his shotgun across his chest in a defensive posture, then raised it toward his shoulder as if to strike her with it. Maggie grabbed the gun and twisted it from his hands in a millisecond. She was as surprised as Bobby was when she got it away from him. Not sure what to do next, Maggie turned and ran toward her house with the gun.

Bobby Clark was dumbfounded. It happened so fast! "I have a gang!" he shouted. "They'll be coming for you. You better bring that back!"

Maggie kept running until she reached her house. She had left the back door unlocked and quickly yanked it open. Safe inside, she slammed the door shut and secured a latch bolt at the top. Then she peeked out a kitchen window, praying he wouldn't come after her. When she was finally satisfied that he wasn't, she flopped down on her couch, exhausted from her ordeal, and fell asleep.

A hard knock on the door jolted her awake. Maggie pulled herself off the couch and peeked around a corner wall into the living room. There was a large picture window by the front door, and she could see a police car parked outside by the curb. Relieved, she went to the door and opened it.

The officer told her that Bobby Clark had stopped by the station to report that she had stolen his shotgun, and asked if that was true. Maggie admitted she took his gun, but when she explained everything, the officer felt that she reacted in self-defense and asked if she wanted to press charges against Clark for aggravated assault or terroristic threats. Maggie told him she did not. All she had ever wanted was for the boy to keep away from her house, but now she wanted him off the property entirely. It wasn't her land, but she knew the owner and was going to tell him what happened. Once he found out, she was sure he'd never allow Bobby Clark to return.

The police officer took Clark's gun back to the station and called the Game Commission. Once again, I was the last person on the scene. But as stated before, such is the life of an urban game warden.

I went to the police station and collected Bobby Clark's shotgun for evidence. Because he was only seventeen, and considered a minor under the law, I dealt directly with his parents. They were surprised to see me at the door with Bobby's shotgun in my hand.

"Game warden!" said the father incredulously. "Why do you have Bobby's gun?"

I stepped inside and explained everything: the confrontations between Maggie and their son over the past several weeks, how she had managed to wrestle his gun away…and why, the verbal threats he hurled at her and the ensuing police investigation. His parents were shocked.

"That doesn't sound like our Bobby at all!" exclaimed his mother. "He would never hit anyone, especially a woman."

The father said he thought the entire matter was preposterous. He refused to believe his son had threatened Maggie.

And therein lies the problem, I thought: overprotective parents who coddle their son and refuse to believe the truth even when it stares them in the face.

"Is this woman pressing charges against our son?" asked the father.

"No," I said. "She just wants him to stay away from the property."

"Absolutely!" said his mother. "I'll make sure he does, too. Our Bobby needs to stay away from that woman before she hurts him!"

"Is your son here?" I asked.

"No," she said. "And even if he was, I wouldn't let him talk to you without a lawyer present."

I said, "I found dozens of empty shotgun shells in the cornfield where the incident took place. I can match them to your son's shotgun if necessary."

"Why are you collecting empty shotgun shells and bothering us with all this?" asked the father. "I thought you said she wasn't pressing charges."

"She's not, but I am. I'm going to file citations against your son for littering and for hunting too close to an occupied building."

"And that will make everything go away?"

"For me it will. The local police won't get involved unless the complainant wants to press charges. Like I said before, she does not, but you need to make sure your son stays away from her property after this."

"You can bet on that," he said. "How much is the fine?"

I told him it would be twenty-five dollars for each offense (this was back in 1976), and he met me later in the week with his son to settle on a field acknowledgement of guilt. Although the case was closed, I worried that Bobby would find himself in more trouble down the road. He was still young, and I hoped that his parents soon realized their son had some serious emotional issues and would secure the professional help he needed to overcome his problem.

Outlaw Trappers

OF ALL THE NUISANCE WILDLIFE COMPLAINTS I dealt with—and there were many thousands—the raccoon (appropriately masked) was far and above the most common. Intelligent, gregarious and mischievous, with front feet that serve as hands, they created more problems for people than all the other critters combined. Experts at rummaging through garbage cans after knocking them over and prying off lids with ease, they would scatter the contents all about as they scavenged for a free meal. Plastic bags made life easy for the masked bandits, the streets in some neighborhoods looking like a cyclone went through after gangs of marauding raccoons had their way with them the night before.

Expert climbers, they would scale exterior walls, rip out attic vents and climb inside to rear their young in spring. Chimneys were another favorite location for pregnant females. After clambering to the top, they would slip inside, hind feet first, and shinny down to the closed damper, spreading their legs from wall to wall for support as they descended.

Because raccoons are highly susceptible to canine distemper and rabies, it wasn't unusual to get a call about a "sick" raccoon at least once per week. Both diseases seemed to be cyclic, with some years being more severe than others. And because distemper and rabies are similar in how they affect raccoons, causing them to stumble around in broad daylight as if drunk, I had to give priority to every call and get there as soon as possible. While distemper is a contagious and serious disease affecting dogs, raccoons, skunks and other mammals, it cannot be contracted by humans. Rabies, however, is a deadly disease for both humans and animals caused by a virus that attacks the nervous system. The virus is secreted in saliva and is usually transmitted by a bite from an infected animal. Rabies can be also be spread when saliva from a rabid animal comes in contact with an open cut on the skin or the eyes, nose, or mouth of a person or animal. Once the outward signs of the disease appear, rabies is nearly always fatal. Rabies most often occurs in wild animals, especially raccoons, skunks, bats and foxes. Free roaming cats are more likely to be infected with rabies than dogs because many cat owners do not bother to vaccinate them.

Let's face it, raccoons are cute, especially the babies. As a result, the young were often sold as pets (illegally) to unsuspecting buyers. Others became pets when someone would find a young raccoon that had fallen from a tree and took it home. It is unlawful to take an animal from the wild in most states, including Pennsylvania, and there were a number of occasions when I had to confiscate a "pet" raccoon from someone after getting a call that a family member had been bitten. In every case, I had to kill the raccoon and submit its head to the Department of Agriculture Laboratory for a rabies examination (this could only be done by examining brain tissue). This is always unpleasant, not only for me, but also for the people who find me at their door with a warrant in my hand.

And then there was the time that I removed four newly born raccoon cubs from someone's chimney only to be called back days later when the owner discovered their mother lying dead in her back yard. As a precaution, I submitted the animal's head to the lab for examination and it came back positive. Because I had handled the cubs without gloves, it was recommended that I get a series of rabies shots. The vaccine was administered over a period of weeks, starting with a syringe that looked as big as a turkey baster. The serum was injected in both cheeks (and not the ones on my face). It went in slow as molasses and was painful, but when the alternative was a slow death accompanied by convulsions and drowning in my own spit or blood, I chose the vaccine. The initial double dose was followed by a more civilized and much less painful weekly series of shots in the upper arm.

Montgomery County was overrun with raccoons because they had no natural enemies other than motorists who would occasionally hit one and kill it. As a result, I was going crazy trying to handle all the complaints. In those days (mid-1970s), there were no nuisance wildlife trappers licensed by the Game Commission like there are today. Fortunately for me, and the thousands of urban dwellers living in my district, fur prices began to increase significantly, rising to highs that hadn't been seen since the early nineteen hundreds. Seventy-dollar foxes and forty-dollar raccoons were unheard of in the past, but by the mid-seventies things changed significantly and the raw fur industry was seeing some of the best years for sales in its long history. Keep in mind that forty dollars in 1975 is equivalent to almost two hundred dollars today. Some men quit their jobs and became fulltime trappers, earning double and triple what they made working a regular job at the mill. Due to record-setting prices for almost all furs, trappers were popping up everywhere. This was good news and bad news for urban game wardens with an overpopulation of raccoons in their districts.

The bad news was that people who had never set a trap before were using improperly placed traps resulting in toe catches. Raccoons that escaped from these traps were often more difficult to catch the second time around. These novice trappers also set traps too close to homes and used bait that attracted pet dogs and cats. Reports of domestic animals with a foot stuck in the jaws of a steel trap gave a black eye to all trappers. The newspapers were having a field day with it, publishing front page photos of someone's beloved pet with its paw all bandaged up at the local animal hospital.

The good news was that many experienced men that had hung up their traps years before due to low fur prices were now returning to the trade. These expert trappers were beginning to make a dent in the large population of raccoons in my district, but they had some major obstacles to hurdle when dealing with the dense human population, not the least of which was the Game Commission's safety zone regulation. By law, trappers had to be more than 150 yards from occupied buildings, but raccoons were living in and around peoples' homes, making it extremely difficult to find suitable places to set traps. However, a number of neighborhoods and business campuses had small streams on their outskirts, which were not in safety zones. These were ideal places to set traps, as raccoons would always hunt for natural foods in these watercourses, using the road culverts and bridges that channeled them to travel to the next location.

Urban trappers often set traps for raccoons at bridges and culverts

Being a lifelong trapper myself, I understood the difficulties facing other trappers in my district, so I didn't spend time patrolling wetlands and vacant fields bordering housing developments or other buildings. After all, these men were making life better for everyone, including me. The exception, of course, was if I received a complaint from a homeowner. Then I had no choice but to respond. If it was a simple safety zone complaint, I would issue a written warning. There would be no fine unless there were extenuating circumstances, like in the three cases that follow.

Lying Larry Fritz

As OFTEN HAPPENED IN MY URBAN DISTRICT, the whole thing started with a call from the police informing me that a witness had contacted them concerning unlawful hunting in a state park where only shotguns could be used. I was told the witness had spotted a man hunting with a rifle, so I proceeded directly to the park, hoping to find him.

While searching the area on foot, I noticed a body-gripping trap set in a waterway loaded with muskrat tracks. Surprisingly, the trap had a metal tag attached to the chain (required by law) with the owner's name and address printed on it. The reason I was surprised, was because muskrat season wouldn't start for another two weeks.

Square-jawed bodygripping trap set in water at center of picture

Most poachers remember to remove their tags when trapping prior to the opening day so their unlawful activity can't be traced back to them. Investigating further, I found evidence showing where another trap had been set and then removed at a narrow underwater muskrat channel. The water in the channel was muddy, indicating a recent catch.

Suspecting the trapper had the muskrat at his home, and that he may have additional furs taken in closed season, I went to the local district justice and applied for a search warrant. The tag on the remaining trap was clear evidence of a Game Law violation in itself, as it had been set prior to the opening day, and because it contained the owner's name and address, I was able to use the information to acquire the warrant.

It took several hours to go through all the necessary paperwork, but as soon as I had the warrant signed by the judge, I traveled directly to the suspect's house. He wasn't home when I arrived, so I parked nearby and waited.

It was almost dark when Larry Fritz pulled into his driveway that evening. He never noticed my patrol car out on the street, and when he opened the driver's door to climb out, he saw me standing by his car. He was taken completely off guard by my presence, but pretended not to be.

"Game Warden!" he said. "A little out of your territory, aren't you?"

Fritz was in his mid-forties with a balding head and squinty eyes that made him look like he was getting ready to sneeze.

"I don't think so," I said. "I'm here to talk to you about your traps."

"Traps?"

"I found one of your traps set at a muskrat run this morning," I said.

"Not *my* trap! Season's not open yet."

"Has your tag on it."

His eyes suddenly widened with the realization that he'd forgotten to remove it. He stared at me in silence for a moment, and I watched his chest begin to deflate. Then: "I guess you got me," he said, shaking his head with regret. "I was setting traps for raccoons when I saw the fresh muskrat sign. Couldn't resist putting a couple traps out."

"Just two traps? You don't have others set?"

"Not for muskrats. But I do have a bunch of coon sets out. Season's open, so no problem there, right?"

"Right," I said. "Do you have any furs in your house or garage?"

"I just started trapping yesterday," he said. "Didn't catch anything yet."

"I want you to open your trunk."

"Not unless you have a warrant. If not, I want you to get off my property."

I reached into my jacket pocket, pulled out my search warrant, and handed over his copy.

Fritz looked at the document, then stared at me in awe. "This says you can search my car, house, outbuildings…everything I own!"

I nodded affirmatively. "Mr. Fritz, I don't want to spend the night rummaging through your property, but I will if I have to. It would be a lot easier if you start cooperating."

Fritz shook his head wearily and walked to the back of his car. "Come on," he said. "No sense trying to fight it."

I walked over and he opened the trunk. There were three dead muskrats inside. I took the carcasses and put them in my patrol car. Walking back I said, "I want to look in your garage, too."

Fritz blew a long sigh. "Okay, I admit I've got furs in there, but you won't find anything in my house or my basement. Honest. I've got everything in my garage." He motioned me to follow him. "Let's get this over with."

I followed Fritz through a side door leading into his garage. He reached over and flipped a switch lighting two large fluorescent lights dangling from a low ceiling. Dozens of steel traps hung from nails on the back wall. More nails protruded from exposed ceiling joists where Fritz hung his pelts on wire fur forms to dry. In all, there were twenty raccoons, five opossums and ten muskrats. He obviously hadn't just started trapping yesterday.

"I'll get the muskrats down for you," he said. He brought a six-foot wooden stepladder from the back wall and set it under the pelts. Then he climbed partway up, removed the muskrat skins from the wire forms, and brought them down. Stepping over to a workbench, he grabbed an empty burlap seed bag and dropped the pelts inside. "No sense getting yourself all greased up," he said, handing me the bag.

I walked outside with him and put the bag of furs in my patrol car along with the three muskrats from before. I told Fritz I wanted to see his basement, too, and he took me into the house and down a flight of steps into the cellar. There were no additional furs or traps, so I went back to my patrol car and wrote citations for trapping in closed season and the possession of thirteen unlawfully killed muskrats. The fine was over two hundred dollars (this was in 1977 and equal to seven hundred dollars today), plus court costs and revocation of his trapping privileges.

It was one of the biggest trapping cases I had in my thirty-two years as a game warden. And it was the only time a trapper who was poaching furs in closed season had left his name and address as a calling card for me. Had Fritz remembered to remove the metal tag from his trap, I might never have known about his illegal trapping activity.

Slamming Sammy Berns

THE PERSIAN CAT IS A MEDIUM SIZED, longhaired breed of cat characterized by its round face and short muzzle. They are a pedigreed cat and cost around $500-$700 depending on the fur color. They are considered an indoor cat, and most people don't let them roam outdoors due to their long hair which must be groomed daily to keep them looking good. Unfortunately for Danny Berger, he allowed his cherished Persian to go outside one day and it never returned.

Danny was alarmed when Kitty didn't come to the back door after being out for several hours. Kitty was the Persian's name, and she always returned within twenty minutes or so. She really didn't like the outdoors, preferring to lounge within the warmth and comfort of her owner's home. But Danny thought it was good for her to get some fresh air and stretch her legs every so often, and he always made sure she got a taste of the outdoors at least once per week.

But when Kitty failed to return, Danny feared the worst. So at daybreak the following morning, he threw on his jacket and hat and started searching for her on foot. His neighbor also had a Persian cat named Fiddles. Fiddles had gone missing last week after being let out to play in the yard. His neighbor thought someone must have taken Fiddles because he always came home after a short romp outside…just like Kitty always had.

Danny walked in circles around his house, gradually enlarging his loop as he ranged farther and farther from his home. When he reached the state road, a hundred yards away, he shielded his eyes from the sun with a hand and looked up and down the highway hoping not to see her lying dead somewhere. Kitty had white fur, and in the distance, he saw a small white lump on the berm where a creek went under the road through a culvert pipe. Danny walked toward the object, his stomach churning as he approached. And the closer he got, the more certain he was that Kitty was dead. At first he thought she'd been hit by a car, but a closer look revealed something else entirely. Her right paw was scarred and her head bashed in. Danny had seen a pickup truck parked along the road next to the creek every morning for the past week and suspected someone was setting traps. Now he was certain, and believed his cat had been caught and killed by the trapper, its body tossed along the berm to look as if it had been struck by a passing motorist. Crushed by the loss of his beloved Persian, he picked her limp body off the macadam road and carried her home.

Trapping season had ended weeks earlier, so when I got the call about a cat that had been caught in a trap, I went directly to Danny Berger's place to examine the Persian's body before he buried it. His instincts were spot on. The cat's paw showed clear evidence that it had been caught in a foothold trap, and I could also see where its head had been hit with a blunt instrument. There was no doubt in my mind that the cat had been killed by a trapper.

The trapping industry was getting enough negative publicity from the myriad of animal rights organizations in those days (and still is today). With the fur boom in full swing, there were more than a few slob trappers around, and it was people like them who helped give trapping a bad name. I needed to catch this outlaw and put him out of business as soon as possible. Fortunately, Danny Berger had copied down the tag number of the suspect's truck days earlier on his way to church.

Suspecting I'd find some traps still set along the stream, I walked over to the spot where Danny found his Persian. Standing along the berm, I looked down at the waterway, probing the streambank with my eyes for a likely place to set traps. Auto traplines were one of the best ways to catch large numbers of raccoons. A trapper could set a hundred traps easily by driving from one bridge or road culvert to another, stopping at each one with a couple of traps in hand. These are key locations for trappers who wish to save time but still cover acres of territory. Because they act as funnels for furbearers, they can be a virtual gold mine to trappers, and I wondered if my suspect had traps set all over the county.

Stream running under road culvert

A glint of sun reflected off something on the brushy streambank ahead. Curious, I stepped down to the water's edge and found an empty can of salmon that had been carelessly tossed aside by the trapper. This was obviously the bait he used for his raccoon sets. The fact that it had been left high and dry on the bank indicated he was an amateur. An experienced furtaker would never have done this. First, it was a littering violation; secondly, it reeked of salmon and would only serve to attract raccoons away from your traps as they crawled up on the bank to investigate the smell. An experienced trapper, after baiting his traps with salmon from the can, would have used the empty container as an attractant in itself. The fishy odor would linger inside for at least a week, and a hole dug into the streambank with the can stuffed inside would catch many a 'coon.

Unfortunately, fish attracts cats too, and experienced trappers operating close to houses wouldn't use it for bait unless the traps were set in a manner that wouldn't catch domestic animals. Danny Berger told me his neighbor's Persian had been missing for a week, and after finding his own cat dead, he suspected the trapper killed both of them. I figured the same thing. The stream ran well within the safety zone of both houses, and because cats are natural hunters with a keen sense of smell, they surely would have been attracted to the salmon.

Certain that some traps had been set nearby, I began walking downstream and soon found where a small hole had been dug into the bank and baited with salmon. A foothold trap had been placed in the shallow water directly in front of the hole. It was a typical raccoon set, and because the water was only an inch deep, it probably would not have stopped a cat from sticking its foot in the trap as it investigated the bait.

I pulled the trap and found it was untagged. No surprise considering it was closed season. After finding only one trap downstream, I walked back to the road and crossed to the other side. Walking upstream, I soon came across another untagged trap that had been set for a raccoon. Both traps had been secured to railroad tie plates with black annealed wire. I pulled that trap as well, and after finding no more, went back to my patrol car and ran the tag number that Danny Berger had taken from our suspect's truck. It came back to an address only five miles away, so I started my engine and drove directly to it.

When I arrived, a pickup truck was parked in the driveway. The license plate matched the one I had, so I started toward the house when the garage door suddenly opened. I stopped by the rear of the pickup truck as my suspect approached. There were several loose railroad plates lying in the bed of the truck and at least a dozen steel traps. They were the same type as the ones that had been set along the stream: size 1½ Victor coilsprings. But because thousands of trappers nationwide used these traps, it wasn't enough for probable cause to arrest him.

"Can I help you, officer?" he asked walking toward me. He was in his thirties, his face covered by a scraggly beard.

"State game warden," I said.

"I see that. What do you want with me?"

"I'd like to start with your name."

"Sammy Berns," he said, sticking out a hand. I didn't bother shaking it.

"Do you have traps out right now?" I asked.

"Nope. Just didn't bother cleaning out my truck when the season closed." He smiled reassuringly. "I'm on the lazy side, that's all."

"Mind if I look around?"

"Go right ahead."

I lowered the tailgate and pulled the traps toward me. One had cat hairs between the jaws, but they did not match the white Persian's. "Catching cats?" I said, holding the trap up so he could see the hairs.

"That's coon hairs, man. Take a good look."

Knowing I couldn't make a case I let it go. "What's in the bucket up front?" I asked.

"That's my bait bucket."

It was in the corner near the outer edge of the bed, so I walked over and lifted it out. There were several sealed cans of salmon inside. I picked one out and examined it. "Hmm, looks familiar," I said.

He smiled weakly. "Why's that?"

"I just left a stream where someone was setting traps with the same brand of canned salmon for bait."

"Lots of guys use that stuff. Not just me. Besides, I ain't trapping."

I pulled out a can and turned it upside down. The bottom had been stamped with a manufacturer's code and expiration date. I showed it to Sammy. "The can I found at the creek has the exact same code number and date on it. I also found two traps: Victor double coilsprings just like yours. Both traps were secured to railroad plates with black annealed wire…just like the roll of wire and railroad plates I see lying in your bed right now."

"Maybe the guy bought his fish at the same store I did."

"Sammy, do you think I'm here because I was just passing by, saw your truck, and decided to look in the bed to see if there were traps inside?"

He shrugged offhandedly. "How should I know?"

"A homeowner—the one whose cat you killed—has seen your truck parked by the stream where I found the traps every morning for the past week. He wrote down your license plate number and gave it to me. That's why I'm here."

Reality began to set in. Sammy knew the game was over. He dropped his head and blew a long sigh. "Okay, they're my traps," he said. "I admit it. But I didn't kill his cat."

I couldn't prove he did, so I focused on the Game Law violations that I knew would stick, and filed charges on him later that day for trapping in closed season, using two untagged traps and for trapping in a safety zone. The fine came to seventy dollars along with the loss of his trapping privileges for a full year.

But some people never learn, and six months after his revocation period ended, I caught him trapping in a safety zone once again (not the same one as before) and using untagged traps. I arrested him on the spot, gave him a hundred dollar fine, and yanked his license for two more years.

Although I never ran into him after that, I don't think he stopped trapping. Instead, I believe he simply moved his trapline into a neighboring county where he'd be less likely to see me again.

Relentless Ronnie Kling

IN MAY 1978, ON THE FIRST DAY OF SPRING gobbler season, I came across Ronnie Kling walking out of the woods with a shotgun in his hand. He was in his mid-twenties, dressed in camouflage with his face painted black to help conceal himself from any sharp-eyed longbeard that might come his way. He stopped dead when he saw me, his mouth agape, shoulders drooping as I walked over to check his license. I was in full uniform, including a badged Stetson hat.

"State Game Warden," I said. "I'd like to check your hunting license."

Ronnie Kling took a step back. "What for?"

"To make sure you have one," I said.

He turned around, but there was no hunting license pinned to his back.

"Where is it?" I asked.

He spun around to face me. "Where's what?"

"There's no license on your back."

Ronnie gave me a phony look of surprise. "Must have lost it back in the woods," he said. "It was there when I left this morning."

I didn't believe him and I didn't have time to play around. It was a busy day with heavy hunting pressure. "Let's see your driver's license," I said.

Ronnie Kling reached into his back pocket, pulled out a wallet and extracted his license for me. I took it from him and jotted down the information on a note pad. "I'll be at the state police barracks in Limerick between two and five today," I said. "I want you to bring your hunting license over so I can see it." (The State Police let me use a room in the barracks to settle cases by field acknowledgements and collect cash fines.)

But Ronnie Kling never showed up that day, so I filed a citation against him for hunting without a license. Kling plead guilty later that week and paid his fine, thinking the matter was over and done; however, the Game Commission later revoked his hunting and trapping privileges for one year and sent him an official notice by registered mail.

But that didn't stop Ronnie Kling.

The following November, one of my deputies was on patrol in the same township where I had caught Kling hunting without a license when he spotted a pickup truck parked along a wooded area posted against trespassing. It was Ronnie Kling, and he had just exited the truck with a steel trap in his hand when he saw the car coming his way. Taking no chances, he tossed the trap into the woods and stood by his truck, hoping the intruder would move on.

Because the deputy was driving his personal car, and it was unmarked, Kling didn't know it belonged to a game warden. His concern was that the car might be the landowner or a nosy neighbor. Since he didn't have permission to be on the property, he got rid of the trap in case they stopped to question him.

The deputy had seen Kling throw something into the woods as he rounded the bend, but he was too far away to tell what it was. Suspecting a littering violation at the minimum, he pulled to the roadside and parked behind Kling's truck. He was in full uniform as he stepped out to question him.

"Do you have permission to be here?" asked the deputy.

Kling said, "I just saw a deer run into the woods, so I pulled over to watch. I'm not hunting."

He walked over to Kling's pickup truck and looked into the cab for firearms. There were none. "I saw you throw something into the woods a few seconds ago. What was it?"

"I didn't throw anything," said Kling. "I just stopped to see the deer."

The deputy knew what he saw, and intended to search for it, but wanted to see the man's identification first, and asked for his driver's license.

Kling pulled out a wallet and handed it to him. The deputy didn't know Ronnie Kling from the man in the moon, and he had no idea that he was on revocation at the time. After recording the information from his driver's license, he asked him, once again, what he threw into the woods.

"I didn't throw anything," insisted Kling.

With that, the deputy walked into the woods and began searching for the object. It took some time, but he finally spotted a rusty steel trap lying on the ground, its reddish-brown color blending so perfectly with the leaf cover that he almost missed it. The trap was untagged, so it would be impossible to prove it belonged to Kling, but the deputy was certain that the trap had been the mystery object he saw Kling toss into the woods, so he picked it up and walked back to him.

"How many traps do you have set here?" he said, showing Kling what he found.

"That's not mine. I was checking traps for a friend and found it lying by the stream, so I picked it up."

"Where's your friend?"

"Home sick with the flu."

"Where are his traps?"

Kling pointed to a stream fifty yards away at the bottom of the woods. "Down by the water."

The deputy escorted Ronnie Kling down to the stream where he found three more traps. They were set for raccoons and none were tagged. After obtaining the name and address of Kling's sick friend, he turned the case over to me for prosecution.

I waited two weeks before contacting Kling's friend, so he'd have time to get well. Besides, I didn't want to risk catching the flu in the middle of hunting season. He admitted that the traps were his and settled on a field acknowledgement of guilt for setting them untagged. Because Kling was on revocation for hunting without a license at the time, it was unlawful for him to assist anyone who was hunting or trapping. So I contacted him about the violation and he signed a field acknowledgement of guilt for trapping while on revocation and paid a forty-dollar fine. In addition to the fine, his hunting and trapping privileges were revoked for two more years.

The following year (October 10, 1979), I encountered Ronnie Kling again. I wasn't looking for him. In fact, I didn't expect to see him at all. He still had a full two years to go before he could legally hunt in Pennsylvania. And after being caught twice before, I thought, at the very least, he'd do his poaching in another county rather than where my deputies and I routinely patrolled. But sure enough, as I cruised along the same road where my deputy caught him checking traps the previous fall, I spotted his pickup truck parked by a grassy area bordering the woods. To say I was surprised would be an understatement. There was no doubt in my mind that it was him and that he was hunting. What would it take to stop the guy? I began to suspect he might have some kind of mental disorder. What else would prompt someone to keep breaking the law, in the same general area, driving the same easily identifiable vehicle, after getting caught twice before? They say the definition of insanity is doing the same thing over and over and expecting different results. Could that have been Kling's problem?

I concealed my patrol car close by and waited for him to come out of the woods rather than go in searching for him. Archery deer season was open, and I suspected he'd be in full camouflage making it extremely difficult to find him. There were other hunters in the area as well, and I didn't want to risk being shot in mistake for a deer. Maybe I was being overly cautious in that regard, but I'd investigated so many hunting accidents where hunters were mistaken for game that I thought it best to stay back. Besides, he'd likely see me long before I saw him once I entered the woods, which would give him a much better opportunity to flee than if I waited for him here.

As darkness began to cover the landscape, I saw two figures emerge from the shadows. Both men were dressed in camouflage clothing. Both men had bows. But as they approached, they hid them in some heavy brush hemming the wooded area. I can't be sure why, only that it might have been a precaution so a passing motorist wouldn't report their unlawful hunting activity.

I started my engine and pulled my vehicle from the shadows, blocking them in. There was no need to identify myself. Kling and I were old acquaintances by now.

I stepped out of my patrol car and walked over to the men. Both stood silently by the tailgate of their truck. They knew I had them dead to rights, but as often is the case, when a suspect has a partner alongside him, it can cause tensions to rise. Even though I was an armed, uniformed officer, well within my rights to inspect both men, it was still two against one. These odds can embolden an outlaw at times, especially if he is under the mistaken impression that he's a marked man, being singled out or hunted down by a vindictive enforcement officer.

"Not you again!" scoffed Kling. "Is that all you do, spend every day looking for me, so you can harass me?"

Ignoring his outburst, I asked to see their hunting licenses (even though Ronnie couldn't legally purchase one, and if he had, I intended to prosecute him for it)

Ronnie Kling's partner turned his back and I pulled his cardboard license from the plastic holder pinned between his shoulders and looked it over. I was surprised to find that the man was Kling's brother, Johnnie. I looked at Ronnie. "Got a license on your back?"

He chuckled at the notion. "Why bother? I'm not allowed to hunt anyway thanks to you!"

I walked over to the bushes where they'd hidden their archery equipment, picked it up and placed everything in my patrol car. Visibility was poor and I kept my eyes locked on both men as I returned to face them. "Johnnie," I said, "you're hunting after hours. That's a violation of the Game Law. The fine is ten dollars."

He nodded, telling me he understood.

I turned to Ronnie. "You're hunting after hours too. But you're also on revocation. Your fine is fifty dollars but you'll also be getting at least three more years added to the loss of your hunting and trapping privileges."

After I said it, I wondered if he cared. He was hunting right now while on revocation. What difference would it make if he got another three years added to his duration?

"Tell you what," he said. "I'll give you a thousand dollars if you get me a license so I can hunt. I'll go home right now and bring the money back (same value as $3500 today)."

"Are you trying to bribe me?" I said, my tone more a warning then a question.

"Call it a gift! Just promise to leave me alone and it's yours."

"I'd call it a felony, not a gift. You need to rethink what you're saying."

Ronnie Kling shook his head in defiance. "Look. It don't matter what you do to me or how long you take my license away. You will never stop me from hunting or trapping. In fact, I'll be back here next year setting traps. Just letting you know right now so you can come looking for me."

I believed him. And it was hard to stand there and listen to the man, knowing I really didn't have a comeback. He was relentless. He had no fear. There was nothing I could say to him. Nothing that would make him respect the law.

"Just tell me where and when," he persisted. "I'll meet you and pay my fine. After that, I'm gonna have my name legally changed so I can hunt any time I want."

"You'll still be in violation," I said. "Why don't you try New Jersey? I hear the hunting is pretty good there."

Ronnie Kling stared at me for a moment, his mouth open in surprise. And to this day, I don't know if I insulted the man or presented him with an opportunity that he never thought of before.

In any case, Ronnie Kling and his brother both paid their fines later that week, and I never saw them again, their absence from my life a "gift" far better than the thousand dollars Ronnie Kling had offered before, and I gladly accepted it.

The Poacher's Son

As many of you know by now, game wardens run into all kinds of people. A small percentage of them are outright lawbreakers who plan their crimes against our wildlife resources well ahead of time, calculating their every move, and can often be found boasting about the big buck or trophy-sized bear they killed to anyone who will listen.

Unfortunately, too many people who overhear them boasting about their illegal kill tend to look the other way. *He probably needs the meat to feed his family*, they falsely believe. Others worry about retaliation, thinking the poacher will shoot them or burn down their house if they report them to the law. It's easy to come up with an excuse when you don't want to get involved. Don't get me wrong: some folks have a valid reason for looking the other way. But without the eyes of the public watching out for us, Pennsylvania's thin green line of game wardens can easily be penetrated.

One thing we can all agree on: poachers are bad news for our wildlife populations, not to mention the lawful hunter. Every deer a poacher kills before the season opens diminishes the opportunity for the honest hunter who goes afield hoping to harvest a nice whitetail. Poachers who shoot deer at night are the absolute worst. The limited visibility after sunset makes their shooting all the more dangerous. A poacher's bullet that misses its target in the dark of night could hit a house that would have been visible in daylight.

But the thing that troubles me most, is when a poacher teaches his children to follow in his shallow footsteps. I've seen it time and again. Sometimes it's the kid who can't seem to smile when I examine the deer he supposedly killed. Dad is right there with him, and claims he's not hunting, just overseeing his son as required by law. The boy, of course, never had a chance. His tag is on the buck, but Dad did the shooting. The thrill of the hunt was never the issue. The important thing (in Dad's mind) was that a deer is to be killed for every license purchased by his family.

I've seen this with road hunters too. We all know it's illegal to drive around looking for a deer you can shoot from the road. Most of these folks (who aren't physically disabled) are just being lazy. But some hunt from their vehicles because they've already taken the legal limit of game and feel they're less likely to be apprehended in the safety of their automobile.

I've met more than a few road hunters who choose to bring a youngster along with them. These kids are brought up with the conception that it's okay to cheat. It's okay to break the law. To compound the scenario, when stopped by a game warden, they are taught not only to lie, but that it's the right thing to do. It's like some bizarre game they're all playing called *Beat the Game Warden*.

One of the saddest examples I've seen happened during the antlerless deer season in Montgomery County many years ago while covering for a game warden in the northern half of the county who was out sick at the time. While my district was in the Special Regulations Area (buckshot only), hunting with rifles and revolvers was legal here. His district had a lot of open land, some of it quite rural, and it was a good opportunity for me to get out of the heavily populated southern half of the county and breathe some fresh air.

I was driving my marked patrol car along a country road with long, grassy meadows on both sides, when I saw two figures standing in the field a good hundred yards away, both were wearing orange vests. As I slowed down for a better look, one turned and ran toward a wooded area in the distance. Suspecting a violation of some kind, I pulled over and started walking toward the remaining subject. The man wasn't carrying a rifle or shotgun, and as I drew near, I looked for a bulge under his clothes that would indicate he might be armed with a handgun. But there was none.

"Who was that with you?" I asked, stepping close to him.

"Nobody," he replied. "Just some guy taking a walk. I don't know his name."

"Why did he run?"

"I don't know."

"And you don't know who he is?"

He shook his head no.

"Are you hunting today?" I asked.

"Nope. Just out for a walk."

"Do you have a hunting license with you?"

"On my back," he said, turning.

I pulled his hunting license from its holder and examined it. The man's name was Steven Baines; he was forty years old and lived close by. "I see the antlerless deer tag is missing. So you already got one, huh?"

"Yesterday," he said.

"Your license is marked as a replacement, too."

"That's right. I lost mine and had to buy another one."

I did not believe him. In fact, I didn't believe anything he told me up to that point. I thought it was more likely that he'd killed a buck and a doe with his first license, used the tags, and then went out and purchased a replacement license so he could kill another doe. Unethical and illegal.

"I don't think you're telling me the truth," I told him. "I'm going to ask you again: who was the person that ran away?"

"I told you, I don't know."

I put his license in my back pocket. "Let's take a walk."

His brow narrowed in confusion. "A walk? Where to?"

"Down to my patrol car so I can take you home."

"What do you want to do that for?"

"I'm going to search your house for illegal game…that and whoever ran off when they spotted my car. I have a feeling I might find him there."

I was bluffing, of course. I couldn't search his house without a warrant, and hoped my gesture would put some pressure on him to tell the truth, which it did.

"It was my son," he said nervously. "You won't find him at my house."

"What's his name?"

"Benny."

"How old is he?"

"He's twelve," he said. "A good boy, too."

"What made him run off like that?"

"He saw some deer over by the woods and wanted to get a closer look."

The man just couldn't stop lying, and it was getting old. Chasing after a band of deer in an open field would only cause them to run away. Common knowledge. No hunter would encourage his son to do that.

"I don't believe you, I said. I nodded toward my patrol car. "I want you to come with me."

"Whoa-whoa-whoa!" he cried. "My wife will have a heart attack if you show up looking for Benny. Okay…I'll level with you: I was after another deer. I had a revolver with me…a .357 magnum. When I saw your car, I gave it to my son and told him to run and hide."

I was sickened by the thought. My own son was almost the same age. And I had a daughter who was three. My wife and I did everything we could to bring them up right. This was especially so with Maryann. She was the perfect mother, devoting every minute of her day to our children. Making sure they grew up knowing right from wrong, good from bad, getting them involved with our church. Now I stood before a man who not only used his son to protect his own skin, but also endangered the boy in the process. The gun was obviously loaded when he ran off, nobody hunts with an empty firearm, suppose he would have slipped and fell? Suppose the gun had gone off? I'd investigated enough hunting accidents to envision that scenario and it made my stomach turn.

"Where did he go?" I pressed.

Steven Baines looked over my shoulder toward the distant woodlot. "He's out there somewhere, I guess. Hiding in the woods. When he gets hungry he'll come home."

His answer angered me. It was one of only a few times in my career that I wanted to punch a game law violator. I disliked him that much. Not because he was a poacher and a liar, but because of the emotional abuse he was putting his son through.

"I'm going to look for him," I said.

"I'll go with you," replied Baines. "He'll come if I call him."

"I don't want your help," I snapped. "Go home."

Steven Baines cocked his head and squinted at me. "You sure?"

"Positive."

"Suits me," he said. Then he turned and walked away without a glance back at me.

I wanted to find the boy. Talk to him. Show him he had nothing to fear from me…or any law enforcement officer for that matter. I wanted to undo the damage his father had done. And I couldn't accomplish that if Steven Baines had come with me.

The wooded area where his father thought Benny would be hiding was a good three hundred yards away. I could see a dim trail of bent grass from his footfalls and started in that direction. I took my time, walking as if I didn't have a care in the world, thinking that if I strode forward with purpose in my steps, he might run off again. When I reached the edge of the woods, I stopped.

"Benny!" I called. "Hello! I'm not going to harm you; I just want to talk."

A crow answered in the distance. It was the only sound I heard. The woodlot wasn't so big that I'd never find him, maybe five acres, but it would be a challenge if he circled back. I called again: "You're not in trouble, Benny. You don't have to run from me." Then I started into the woods, stopping every few minutes to look for anything unusual that could lead me to the boy. I have to admit, the thought that a bullet might come my way played in my mind. He had a gun…a very powerful gun, and I was well aware that boys who were scared and who felt threatened have been known to overreact.

When I reached the center of the woods, I saw a rocky outcropping ahead—a mound of heavy boulders in the middle of the all the trees, as if they'd fallen out of the sky. Remnants from a prehistoric age. If I were Benny, that's where I'd be.

There was something about the rocky wall that gnawed at your curiosity, that pulled you toward it. I was hoping Benny was there, that he hadn't run off, that he was waiting for me. I walked around the perimeter until I reached the opposite side and saw him sitting against the cold granite wall, arms folded around bent legs, holding them close to his chest, deep in thought it seemed. I stood and stared at him in silence, as if a single word might send him scurrying like a frightened rabbit.

After a moment, he looked up at me. "I waited for you," he said.

"That's good," I said. "I'm glad."

"I'm not afraid."

I smiled reassuringly. "I can see that. I'm Officer Wasserman, by the way."

"You're a game warden."

"That's right."

The boy stood straight up, as if his knees were steel springs. *Ah! To be young again!* I thought.

"I have a gun," he said.

"I know."

He chinned to his left. "It's behind the big rock."

There was a boulder the size of a truck engine lying nearby. I walked over and looked behind it. A Smith and Wesson .357 Magnum revolver lay there. I picked it up and emptied six live rounds from the cylinder. "Your father gave you the gun, told you to run away," I said. "None of this is your fault."

The boy nodded solemnly. "Is he going to jail?"

"No, but he'll have to pay a fine."

He nodded thoughtfully. "My dad is a good man," he said. "He just doesn't always obey your hunting rules."

"They're not *my* hunting rules, Benny," I said. "They're everyone's. They help keep our deer herd at a healthy level and promote fair play." I paused for a moment, then said, "Do you play sports in school?"

He smiled. "Baseball."

"Three strikes and you're out, right?"

"Yep."

"How would you feel if the schools you were playing against were allowed four strikes?"

Benny frowned. "It's against the rules. It wouldn't be fair!"

"It's important to play by the rules, then, isn't it?" I said. "That way everybody gets a fair shot."

He thought about what I said. Then: "One deer, not two or three. That's what you mean, right?"

"Exactly."

I let it go. Benny loved his father and it would only cause hard feelings between the boy and me if I pushed it. Just what I didn't want. "Come on," I said. "I'll take you home."

We walked out of the field side-by-side, the sun shining on our backs. Benny asked me a lot of questions about my job and what it was like to live the life of a game warden. He seemed relieved that the situation was coming to an end, and that his father wasn't going to jail. When we reached my patrol car, Benny's eyes lit up: the glossy green paint, the colorful door decals, the emergency lights on the roof. He was practically mesmerized and couldn't wait to climb inside to see everything. I started the engine and activated the siren: *Whoop-whoop-whoop!* it wailed. He loved it. He watched intently as I took the mic from my two-radio and reported that I was back in service.

"*Ten-four,*" the dispatcher returned.

"Wow!" he said. "I would love to drive a car like this one day!"

"Maybe you will," I told him. "Pay attention in school and stay out of trouble. If you do, the future is yours."

It was a short drive to Benny's house. When we got there, I walked to the front door with him and knocked. His father opened it and told Benny to go inside while we talked.

I waited until his father stepped outside and closed the door behind him. "I'm going to file a charge against you for attempting to kill a second deer," I said. "The fine is five hundred dollars."

"Fair enough," he said. "Can I have my gun back?"

"When the case is settled," I told him. "Until then, I'll hold it for evidence."

He nodded that he understood and I turned and walked away.

I never saw his father again, but Benny and I met many times after that day. As it turned out, Benny was quite the athlete, and I coached for his Little League baseball team and other sports he played while growing up. He became a fine young man, was deeply religious, and married a wonderful woman. Maryann and I were invited to the wedding and made sure we were there to support Benny and his new bride in their future lives.

I don't know if my interaction with Benny had anything to do with how he turned out in life, but I like to think that it did. As a state game warden, I always tried to be aware of the impact I might have on the people around me, especially the younger ones. I grew up with a deep love of the outdoors, and can't imagine what my life would have been like without the opportunity to go hunting, trapping and fishing. That's why I always tried to protect our hunting heritage and help others to have the same connection with wildlife that I had as a boy. I think I did that with Benny Baines as well as a number of other young people throughout my career, and I will be eternally grateful for the opportunities I had to make a difference in their lives.

Author's Note

After 13 years in Montgomery County, I transferred to Wyoming County in northeastern Pennsylvania. It was here that I spent the remainder of my 32-year career. Stay tuned, faithful reader, there are more stores to come.

William Wasserman, a third-degree black belt in the Korean martial art of *Tang Soo Do* and a former national bodybuilding champion, has written ten books about his life as a state game warden. He received numerous awards for his work in wildlife conservation, including the United Bowhunters of Pennsylvania Game Protector of the Year Award, Pennsylvania Game Commission Northeast Region Outstanding Wildlife Conservation Officer, National Society Daughters of the American Revolution Conservation Medal, and the Pennsylvania Trappers Association Presidential Award. Wasserman has been published in several national magazines including *Black Belt, Pennsylvania Game News, Fur-Fish-Game, South Carolina Wildlife, International Game Warden,* and *The Alberta Game Warden*. Wasserman retired from the Pennsylvania Game Commission after thirty-two years of dedicated service and lives in South Carolina with his wife, Maryann.

POACHER HUNTER

WILLIAM WASSERMAN

TRACK OF THE
POACHER

WILLIAM WASSERMAN

Made in the USA
Columbia, SC
28 April 2025